Theresa,
        Hope this
you to play for pleasure!
        Love,
          Dad & Mum

# Playing the Piano
# for Pleasure

by

*Charles Cooke*

GREENWOOD PRESS, PUBLISHERS
WESTPORT, CONNECTICUT

10 9 8 7 6

# CONTENTS

## Contents

# Preface

PLAYING the piano is my greatest joy, next to my wife; it is my most absorbing interest, next to my work. Therefore I believe I can safely hold that it stands, in relation to my life as a whole, just where a beloved hobby should stand.

I am thirty-six. Twenty-six of these years have been brightened and enriched by music. That is why this book is frankly intended as inspirational. In it I have tried to communicate my indelible enthusiasm for music —in particular for the infinitely varied music that can be drawn from that noble, self-sufficient instrument, the piano. It is a personal book, for the field open to the amateur pianist is so vast that any book on the subject can only tell of the adventures of one amateur who has happily and busily roamed this field. It is my hope that my experiences may provide food for thought and action to three great groups: adults who have played the piano all their lives but would like to improve and expand their playing; adults who studied the piano in their youth, gave it up, and would now like to resume; and adult beginners.

One evening recently, after finishing my regular daily hour of piano practice, I had a sudden startling awareness of the hundreds of thousands of men and women who, like me, love music and love to play the piano; and who, like me, would like to play the piano more and better all the rest of their lives. So I decided to assemble my ideas on this subject—together with the written and the spoken ideas of master pianists and master teachers which I have found illuminating, inspiring, and concretely useful. You hold the result in your hand. I hope with all my heart that you will like it and find it useful. If you play, or used to play, it provides a plan for improving and expanding your playing—a workable plan—a plan which *has* worked, for me. If you do not play but would like to, a teacher is of course essential, but the value to you of this book should increase in proportion to the progress you make. (Some suggestions on selecting a teacher will be found in Appendix A.) I suggest that adult beginners read the short first part—"Goals"—for a quick view (it will pleasantly surprise them, I think) of the achievements that amateur pianists may reasonably aspire to; and I suggest that these adult beginners return later on to read the longer second part—"Means." To any who may feel that mature years are too late to begin piano study, I should like to quote one opinion: "The age of the student is immaterial. Provided there is gift and intelligence, age need not stand in your way. If you are endowed with strong musical gifts in the abstract, you will achieve results superior to those attained by younger people with less talent." Those are the words of Josef Hofmann.

I was ten years old when, in my home in Cooperstown, N. Y., I first began to listen intently to my sister, Lucy E. Cooke, who, then as now, played the piano beautifully. For example, her playing of Beethoven's *Pathétique* Sonata invariably put me in an emotional mist. To be able to play that sonata seemed to me one of the most worth-while and glamorous achievements a human being could aspire to—a view I still hold. When I was eleven, an indulgent uncle made me a Christmas present of piano lessons. I enjoyed everything about them but the practicing, except during a fortunate period when my teacher was Katherine Ruth Heyman, who was then head of the music department of the Knox School in Cooperstown. Throughout my two years with this distinguished artist, who is world-famous for her interpretations of the music of Scriabin, I enjoyed even the practicing! During college and the first half of the sixteen years I have lived in New York City, my interest in piano study dozed, only to awaken suddenly and permanently eight years ago when I had the unusual good fortune of being accepted as a private pupil by James Friskin, noted concert pianist and member of the faculties of the Institute of Musical Art and the Juilliard Graduate School.

In 1930, I joined the staff of *The New Yorker* as a reporter. That has been my bread-and-butter job ever since. More interesting work cannot be found on this planet, I imagine, and to me the most interesting part of it has been interviewing master pianists for stories in *The New Yorker*'s "Talk of the Town." For *The New Yorker*'s whimsical needs, I invariably grill pianists about their hobbies. I have learned that Hofmann is never happier than when inventing in his own machine shop, that Horowitz likes to drive his Rolls Royce at a terrific clip, that Rosenthal plays chess and ponders metaphysics, that Schnabel swims and plays tennis, and that Brailowsky reads, in the original, the masterpieces of Dostoevski, Balzac, and S. S. Van Dine. But—and here I make you privy to a secret my *New Yorker* editors don't know—I also invariably grill pianists for pointers which, though useless for the resultant untechnical story, are highly useful to me for *my* hobby. And therefore useful to every reader of this book, for I have taken pains to include every one of these pointers.

I have purposely placed repertoire first and technique second in this book, reversing the order necessary for those who are studying to be professionals but tending to increase, I believe, the enjoyment to be had from progressive piano study as a hobby. Not that technique as such is slighted: the very method which I recommend for consolidating and expanding your repertoire, i.e., the setting of musical "fractures," is technical drill of a high order—and very functional, as the architects say, for the material it uses is the substance of the compositions themselves. Furthermore, you will find a lot of material on scales, arpeggios, and special exercises —enough to work with for years. But it's music first, and mechanics second, throughout the book. Remember, you amateurs are more fortunate in your playing than most professionals are in theirs. For you there is no grim grind of practicing; no exhausting burden of responsibility; no fierce competition; no endless facing of audiences regardless of the condition of auditoriums, acoustics, or the state of your soul. For you the work is pleasure, as all hobby work is by its nature; the results a satisfaction to yourself, your fellow hobbyists, and such sympathetic listeners as you may find. There need be only one hour of work a day—surely a modest allotment of time to give to a hobby. Of course if you wish to (and can) increase this daily stint, by all means do so.

This, however, I *know:* by systematically working one hour a day at the piano, you can, in a few years, revolutionize your playing.

Have you ever stopped to think what an enormous host we amateur pianists are? Unquestionably more amateur musicians play the piano than any other instrument—probably more than all other instruments combined. Think of the homes you know which harbor a piano. Then think of the homes you know which harbor a violin, cello, viola, flute, clarinet, harp, or a good voice. For generations, the piano has been the standard musical instrument of the home throughout the world; and today the popularity of the piano is the greatest in history. Piano sales in the United States are now at their all-time high: more than one hundred and fifty thousand pianos are purchased every year in this country alone. Olin Downes, music critic of *The New York Times*, recently wrote: "I am certain that the piano has an immense future before it, a future that will be richer, musically speaking, than the past of this most popular and useful of all musical instruments."

Every piano, upright or grand, long owned or newly bought, is literally a treasure chest, waiting to give forth its inexhaustible gifts, to elevate and enrich the lives around it. No truer words have ever been spoken than those of Anton Rubinstein, when, in the fullness of his years and wisdom, he said: "The piano is a lovely instrument. You must fall in love with it, with its sound, and then be tender with it to make it, in turn, be sweeter to you. Herein"—and he laid his hand on the piano— "lies divine beauty."

# PART ONE

## *GOALS*

# 1

# The Place of Music in the Life
# of the Amateur

AMONG my other duties on *The New Yorker*, I am
that magazine's "Mr. Stanley," who explores obscure
islands, and streets with names like Fteley Avenue and
Yznaga Place. This has naturally led me into many im-
probable situations, not to say dilemmas. But nothing in
my decade of reporter's experiences can compare, from
the standpoint of the sheerly fabulous, with some of the
hobbies I've seen.

I have interviewed a man who memorized the location
and gist of every advertisement in each issue of *Collier's;*
he was of course kept as busy discarding this appall-
ingly useless knowledge as acquiring it, for he had to
clear his brain each week to get ready for the next issue.
I have interviewed a man who lived in one room of an
eight-room apartment, the other seven being suffocat-
ingly filled with pulp magazines; he subscribed to every
pulp magazine in America, never read a line of them,

but, in inverse ratio to the tragic draining of his pocket-book, was gradually being engulfed, as Mickey Mouse, the latter-day *Sorcerer's Apprentice*, was engulfed by water. I have interviewed an estimable, white-haired lady who enjoyed riding a scooter as a girl and therefore implacably rode a scooter right up the years to her seventies—often scooting expertly across the Brooklyn Bridge, up Broadway to her bank at Fifty-seventh Street, and back across the bridge to her Brooklyn home. I have interviewed a doctor whose hobby was writing sonnets and who, at the time of the interview, had turned out over fifty thousand, some of them astonishingly fine; the good doctor could no more stop writing sonnets than you and I can stop blinking our eyes, yet he was an eminent psychiatrist whose specialty was treating other people's compulsions!

I mention these instances because they are obviously hobbies that got out of hand. I do not believe in letting a hobby get out of hand. I believe in a balanced diet of (primarily) work and (secondarily) hobby. Nevertheless, these extreme cases hold a lesson: they demonstrate, extravagantly, what the driving force of a powerful sustained interest can produce. But we should always rule our hobby and never let it rule us. Our preoccupation with the piano should be temperate, intelligently controlled and proportioned to our lives as a whole.

One hour a day—held to consistently, never omitted unless circumstances absolutely force an omission—will work wonders. Practicing an hour, then missing three days, then practicing three hours to "catch up," and so on, is by comparison woefully less efficient than the easier routine of one steady, habitual hour through the years. An hour, of course, of concentration, during which you clear your mind of extraneous thoughts; during which you hear, and judge, every tone that you produce as though somebody else had produced it. I believe in quality rather than quantity in piano practice —an hour of concentrated, efficient work rather than a longer period during which the mind, though the fingers continue to drum, goes hazy if not blank. Don't misconstrue my harping on one hour as meaning that sixty minutes a day, however well planned and commendably carried through, are all you should spend at the keyboard. I am referring to one daily hour of *work*—if you can give the name of work to the spectacle of a hobbyist blissfully riding his hobby. Naturally, the more you also *play*—for yourself, for others, with others—the better. The goal of your daily hour should be this and only this: to play the piano better and better from month to month and year to year.

The better you play, the more your circle of friends will expand. You can count on this as confidently as you can count on the sun rising. Music is a powerful magnet which never fails to attract new, congenial, long-term friends.

The place of music in the life of the amateur pianist should be, as I see it, important but not all-important: a source of pleasure in the work done and in the results achieved; above all, a constantly expanding source of beauty and of what can best be called "fineness."

Europe, in the long, fertile period after its first Dark Age and before its Second (or current) Dark Age, spawned thousands of amateurs of music. They were, in the exact translation of the phrase, "lovers of music," but they also played with almost professional skill. Prince Nicholas Esterházy, Haydn's patron, was an expert performer on the baryton, or viola di bordone. Many noble Russians prided themselves on their skill as pianists; Vassili Rachmaninoff, father of the great pianist, for instance. Typical of the European attitude toward amateur music-making was the remark attributed by Mark Hambourg to Fouquet, Louis XIV's minister: "How, Monsieur," said Fouquet to a member of the court who was not an amateur, "you care not for music? You do not play the clavecin? I am sorry for you! You are indeed condemning yourself to a dull old age!" On another continent in another century, the most accomplished amateur pianist in the city of Caracas was one Manuel Antonio Carreño, Minister of Finance of Venezuela and the father of a little girl named Teresa.

Today, of course, we have so far outdistanced Europe in opportunities for *hearing* good music that the Old Countries aren't even in the race any more. Take a typical Sunday, you music lovers who live in and around New York City within earshot of WQXR: by turning your radio dial to that incomparable station, and to the big network stations, it is possible to hear, in the period from early morning until midnight, half a dozen complete symphonies, four or five concertos, three or four symphonic poems, oratorios, cantatas, an entire Mass, an entire opera, a dozen assorted piano, violin, cello, or song recitals, and many quarter-hours and half-hours of chamber music. The nation as a whole, beyond WQXR's benign range, has, among other regularly scheduled musical banquets, the NBC Symphony Orchestra, the Sunday-afternoon Philharmonic from Carnegie Hall, and the Saturday-afternoon Metropolitan opera. Now, in all honesty and all national modesty, where else on the surface of the globe or in the pages of recorded history has there been such an embarrassment of musical riches? Available, mind you, not by going to a concert hall or gathering a group of amateurs in a home, but by the simple operation of twisting a dial. Add to this today's tremendous boom in recorded music and you'll realize (if you hadn't realized it before) that Europe, even in her musical heyday, never offered anything remotely to compare with America's present opportunities for hearing music.

A natural and inevitable result of the recent revolutionary increase in fine music on the radio and in records has been a great increase in personal music-making. This satisfies the urge, deep within us, to make music ourselves—an urge as old as the day when *Pithecanthropus erectus*, strolling through the Javanese sunshine, first whistled a ditty. "How much more satisfying," thought *Pithecanthropus erectus*, startled and pleased, "than just lazily listening to the music of all these Paleolithic birds!" "How much more satisfying," think we as we play the piano or violin or sing, "than just lazily twisting a dial or putting a record on a turntable!" There is in Chicago a Business Men's Orchestra, with a personnel consisting of presidents and vice-presidents of businesses, doctors, dentists, and lawyers. For several years the National Broadcasting Company carried a program called "Music Is My Hobby," originated and produced by Walter E. Koons, himself a gifted amateur pianist. On this program, among other performers, Einstein and Hendrik van Loon played the violin, a vice-president of the Commercial National Bank and Trust Company sang songs, and Hartwell

Cabell, a cousin of Branch Cabell, played the piano.

I have reserved for last a tabulation of some accomplished amateur pianists, because I believe it will both surprise and inspire you: Mr. Cabell, mentioned above; the two Katharines of the stage, Hepburn and Cornell; Maurice Evans, the great "Richard II"; Hollywood's Fred Astaire, Adolphe Menjou, and Charlie Chaplin (Chaplin and Einstein both play the piano in addition to the violin); Vladimir Karapetoff, professor of electrical engineering at Cornell and considered the greatest man in his profession since Steinmetz; Edouard Herriot, thrice Premier of France; Richard L. Simon * of Simon and Schuster; Major John A. Warner, Superintendent of the New York State Police, who recently played Rachmaninoff's First Concerto with the New York City Symphony Orchestra at Carnegie Hall; Rear Admiral R. E. Bakenhus, U. S. N., retired; Peter Arno, the cartoonist; Fritz Kreisler, the violinist; Elliott Paul, the repatriated expatriate writer; and authors Manuel Komroff, John Erskine, Robert Nathan, John Selby, J. B. Priestley, and H. L. Mencken.

We should ponder these words of Ignace Jan Paderewski:

"Music, the most beautiful of arts, will always have

---

* Publisher's note: Delete.
　Author's note: Stet.

its fascination as well as its educational benefits. Music is one of the greatest forces for developing breadth in the home. Far too many students study music with the view to becoming great virtuosi. Music should be studied for itself. The intellectual drill which the study of music gives is of great value—there is nothing that will take its place. And, in addition, the study of music results in almost limitless gratification in later life in the understanding of great musical masterpieces."

The better we can play, furthermore, the better we can browse. I recommend a long life of musical browsing. Albums are especially rich in browsing material and you will find in Appendix A a list of albums of music for the piano. Browse among the pages of piano music as a hungry cow browses in a field. Browse in order to increase your familiarity with piano literature. Browse in order to find new pieces to study. Browse in order to play over such parts as you can manage in masterpieces which taken as a whole are beyond your technical grasp. Browse in order to pass the time away. Browse in order to enjoy yourself. Browse in order to browse.

# 2

# Climbing Higher on the Ladder
# of Piano Literature

I SEE piano literature as a great ladder, each rung like a shelf—a miser's shelf packed with hoarded riches. This is a conservative conception, for not even the symphonic repertoire surpasses that of the piano. If one said *"Eroica"* or "the Fifth," I would make obeisance —and then I would say *"Appassionata"* or "Opus 111." To "Mozart's Jupiter Symphony" I would reply "Chopin's B-minor Sonata"; to "Brahms' First," "Schumann's Fantasia in C." This amiable colloquy could go on for hours; I would not run short of masterpieces first.

And therein lies the challenge and the inspiration to the amateur pianist. Masterpieces lie on every shelf, from the lower rungs to the highest, from the technically simple to the technically forbidding, along with a profusion of lesser but still outstanding compositions. At whatever rung you stand, you will want to linger— working, browsing, enjoying—as you gather skill to ascend unhurriedly to the next rung; then, after a due pause of new work, browsing, and enjoyment, to the next. And so on, as high as you are able, or wish, to go.

Consider some of the lower rungs. Do the mighty torrents of *Götterdämmerung*'s closing pages or the final paean of Beethoven's Ninth Symphony contain more beauty, except in dimension, than Chopin's Prelude in A, No. 7 in Opus 28? Moriz Rosenthal, one of the great technicians of all time, told me that he has studied this brief, simple masterpiece for sixty years and is still finding deeper levels of beauty in it. I venture that no one of my readers who has heard Rosenthal play the Prelude in A will ever forget the experience. This flawless work lies well within the technical grasp of every amateur who has passed the elementary stage of playing; immortal on its staves of cold print, it waits to be brought alive, to be studied and loved for a lifetime by countless pianists, professional and amateur, now and in generations to come.

I want to speak here at some length of Schirmer's *Master Series for the Young*, selected and edited by Edwin Hughes. It is impossible to praise this series too highly: no better gateway to the best in piano music exists. These volumes contain compositions by twelve masters, one volume to each composer—Bach, Handel, Haydn, Mozart, Beethoven, Schubert, Weber, Mendelssohn, Schumann, Chopin, Grieg, and Tchaikovsky. Why this series is not only incomparable but invaluable is best indicated by an excerpt from Mr. Hughes' preface: "Each volume contains a collection of the technically easiest compositions of the composer represented, arranged progressively with regard to difficulty. The numbers included were all penned especially for the instrument by their composers, so that the edition contains none of the tasteless arrangements from operas, symphonies, string quartets, and so on, which have disfigured many publications of like nature in the past." Each volume also contains a short biography of the composer of that volume. The *Master Series for the Young* may be used by the adult amateur in the earlier stages of his development with all the benefits that younger students derive from it. From the point of view of musical taste alone, this series is a triumph. Perusal of the volumes will show you, by the way, that many of the compositions included are well up into the intermediate grades of difficulty. I cite Mozart's Rondo in D, Haydn's Sonata in G, Bach's Gavotte and Musette in G minor, and the Schubert Impromptu in A flat.

I also recommend a series called *The Hundred Best Short Classics,* edited by Cuthbert Whitemore and selected by a committee consisting of Mr. Whitemore, Harold Samuel, Tobias Matthay, and others. No one of the hundred classics included is longer than three pages and each is prefaced by a brief, expert, and provocative note. Paterson's Publications, Limited, of London, are the publishers, but the series may be bought, of course, through Schirmer's. There are seven volumes.

The *Master Series for the Young* and *The Hundred Best Short Classics* provide the finest material available for your early adventures among the works of the great masters. Wilhelm Bachaus, who, like Rosenthal, is possessed of a prodigious technique, once said: "Why seek difficulty when there is so much that is quite as beautiful and yet not difficult? Why try to make a bouquet of oak trees when the ground is covered with exquisite flowers?" That, with an exception, is the point of view from which this book is written. The exception I make is this: we amateurs, as time goes on and our ability increases, will not be content with picking exquisite flowers. We will also uproot shrubs, bushes, saplings—and occasional trees which, if not oaks, will nevertheless be respectably large. What Bachaus calls oaks are, of course, such heaven-storming compositions as Beethoven's *Hammerklavier* Sonata, Liszt's *Don Juan Fantasy*, Balakirev's *Islamey*, the Brahms-Paganini Variations—compositions to tax to the limit the resources of artists who can pluck bouquets of oak trees with ease and carry them with grace—Hofmann, Horowitz, Brailowsky, Simon

Barer, Egon Petri, Bachaus himself. The wise amateur does not tug at oaks, let alone try to uproot them. He leaves them without regret to the master pianists; he is thankful that there are artists who can not only play but interpret them, while he sits back comfortably and listens.

The wise amateur is kept quite busy enough selecting the treasures which, by dint of persevering industry, he can make his own. Such as, to mention a few fine compositions in the intermediate and upper-intermediate grades: Schumann's *Arabeske*, Palmgren's *May Night*, Chopin's Nocturne, Opus 72, No. 1, Debussy's *Clair de lune* and *La Fille aux cheveux de lin*, Liszt's *Consolation* No. 3.

Take careful note of the above, even if some of them seem, just now, beyond your grasp. I am an amateur like you; through the years I have practiced only an hour a day; five years ago, I looked at the music of Chopin's B-minor Scherzo and was dismayed. I was convinced that it was hopelessly and forever beyond me. I kept on working. Today I play it.

Once your feet are planted firmly on the great ladder of piano literature, you will want to climb; if you have already climbed, you will want to climb higher. And you can do it, regardless of the fact that you are no longer "taking lessons." You can do it if you follow, faithfully, the simple suggestions which you will find in this book. Vladimir de Pachmann said: "No worthy teacher expects his pupils to stop with his instruction; the best teacher is the one who incites his pupils to penetrate deeper and learn new beauties by themselves. No one could possibly believe more in self-help than I do."

## 3

## Final Objectives

PLEASE dwell again, for a moment, on that metamorphosis of the B-minor Scherzo from the seemingly unattainable to the attained. To me it is an exciting case history, which focuses the purpose and (if you'll pardon the word) the message of this book. Steady, day-by-day work is what finally brought this masterpiece within my grasp. It is beside the point that I was born with little natural talent for the piano, and that my memory is a weak one which has to be bolstered with every memory aid I have been able to borrow or devise; we are talking about work here—the joys of hobby work, the satisfactions that hobby work brings. Mark Hambourg wrote: "It is a wonderful feeling to notice power growing gradually, and things becoming easy which at first seemed insurmountable." My profoundly gratifying experience with the Scherzo was repeated with other compositions—Chopin's Nocturne in F sharp and *Berceuse*, Debussy's *Reflets dans l'eau*, and Manuel de Falla's *Ritual Fire Dance*, to mention four. It will be repeated with more, I hope, until my fingers are too senile to press down a key. But that doesn't mean you'll ever catch me tugging at an oak.

A good way to start your climb up the ladder is to choose some composition which you have always wanted to play but have felt was "beyond" you. Then work on it along the lines I will suggest in full detail in the second half of this book; work on it until it is yours. The time required will surprise you by its shortness, I think. Then choose another composition; then perhaps two at once. Add one more and you will have a group of five. Keep them all going—don't let three of them fade because you are concentrating on two. How to manage this? You will see presently. Perhaps in that first group you will want to include two or three out of the many pieces you "used to play" but have forgotten. What a host of ghosts of "forgotten" pieces lurk in the memories of all of us who ever studied the piano! Well, re-animate two or three ghosts and include them in your first group; they will make that group easier to achieve. The forgotten-ness of those pieces will turn out to be only partial. Any piece once learned, even if it was learned twenty years ago, is easier to memorize and retain than a new piece of equivalent difficulty. Tobias Matthay, one of the greatest of piano teachers, wrote in his book *On Memorizing:* "One cannot say that an impression once made ever completely fades from the tablets of the mind."

If you set yourself a goal—say, five memorized pieces —and achieve it, you stand on a higher elevation which enables you to see your next possible goal—ten pieces. So . . . when you have five pieces in hand, start another five. This process may be repeated until you startle yourself, as I startled myself in 1938, with a group of twenty-five compositions. Here let me state again that my memory is painfully subaverage; that is why you will find so much material on memory aids in Part Two. I have always had memory trouble. You probably won't have half the trouble with memorizing that I have. But use the "aids," when you come to that part of the book; they will aid good memories as much as poor ones.

To get back to your projected repertoire, a group of twenty-five compositions can be doubled. Did you say it can't? I say it can. Given steady, conscientious work, it certainly can. Of course by the time you have fifty pieces in your active repertoire you will have to practice more than an hour a day. You might even have to practice two hours a day. But you'll be having such a good time with your hobby then that you'll insist on increasing your practice time. Matters might come to such a pass that it will take a team of wild horses—or an irate wife or husband—to get you away from the piano. . . .

"Stop!" you shout. "You are trying to turn me into the man with seven rooms full of pulp magazines!" Well, I'm not—but to prove I'm no extremist, I'll agree to keep our present objective down to twenty-five pieces. Or fifteen, if you prefer. Or ten. Or five. The number of pieces you memorize is up to you; far more important is the improvement in your playing that will come from thorough memorizing and retaining. As a matter of fact, your groups of five or ten pieces needn't be kept at the tips of your fingers at all times, unless you want to do it for the sake of the discipline. It is a very good idea to let a group of pieces lapse for several weeks or even months; when you come back to them, you will be amazed—assuming that you have been working in the meanwhile on other pieces—at the ease with which you can bring them back. Yes, back to the condition which Anton Rubinstein used to tell his pupils was his ideal of a well-learned piece: "A free walk on firm ground."

Now why this emphasis on building a repertoire when we are thinking in terms of general all-round improvement in your playing? You think that repertoire should not be overstressed. True. But repertoire should be *stressed,* for memorizing and retaining pieces lifts the general level of playing faster than any other one thing, through developing so many different things: technical ability, touch, ease and confidence, familiarity on the printed page and on the keyboard with recurring passage-work patterns and chord sequences, and so on. All these contribute toward better sight reading, better accompanying, better ensemble playing, better browsing —better piano playing. As to the work involved, we piano hobbyists might as well face here and now the stimulating fact that there is no field in which more work is waiting to be done: tiring work, refreshing work, exciting work, rewarding work.

I have been talking too long about our goals. Let us turn to the means by which we shall achieve them.

# PART TWO

# *MEANS*

# 1

# Materials

WE WILL need certain materials:

**One piano, tuned.** If your piano hasn't been tuned recently, please have it done. This is a wise prelude to the process of reconstructing your playing, worth much more than the few dollars it costs. I know from experience how we gradually get used to the drooping pitch of neglected piano strings; we can get so used to it that we are astounded, when we finally have our piano tuned, at the round richness of its tones and overtones. We never tolerate for long a yowling radio or a wobbly phonograph turntable, but we are inclined to be complacent about an untuned piano. Tuning should be at regular intervals. I recommend three tunings a year.

**One keyboard, clean.** The relationship between fingers and keyboard is an intimate one. Playing with clean hands on a clean keyboard is an excellent habit to form right at the start. Do you perchance think the point too trivial to bother about? Josef Hofmann doesn't. He wrote: "But before you touch the piano, let me suggest one very prosaic little hint: wash the keyboard as clean as you did your hands."

**One pair of hands.** Fingernails trimmed short enough, please, to allow playing without clicking.

**One hour.** You may have heard me mention this before! How to subdivide this hour will be told in the next chapter. If you ask how, as busy as you are, you will be able to set aside an hour, I answer in the words of Arnold Bennett, the Old Master in the Art of Getting Things Done: "Clear a space for it." Get up half an hour earlier and do half an hour in the morning. Do the other half-hour between the end of your day's work and dinner; or, if you need to rest then, do it after dinner. Or do the whole hour in the morning or in the evening. Or chink in your hour in fragments, if circumstances force you to; whenever you can, as best you may. Arnold Bennett, besides writing an average of 375,000 words a year of fiction, plays, and articles; and learning several languages; and walking six miles a day; and reading an incredible number of books, magazines, and newspapers; and keeping a *Journal* that ran to over a million words; and dabbling in epicureanism, cycling, yachting, billiards, water colors, sketching, and the illumination of manuscripts—in addition to all this, Arnold Bennett practiced and played the piano expertly all his life. How did he find time? He cleared a space.

**One will to work, as far as it is possible, every day.** This is the heart of my system. The surprising results I prophesy are rooted in *one hour done every day*. Daily, it is only one part in twenty-four. But over a period of a year it is 365 hours. And it quickly becomes a habit. Adults enjoy practicing, if they can follow a planned routine which leads to steady improvement. In today's world, people need the outlet of a constructive hobby more than ever before; there is no more enriching hobby than music; to my prejudiced view, there is no better music hobby than playing the piano.

**One will to concentrate while practicing.** You will get more done in less time, in proportion to your concentration. It keeps you from being bored, too; the minutes fly. Your ability to concentrate will improve with use.

**Music.** A gratifying part of the process of revivifying your playing will be the digging up out of your music library of pieces you used to play. These long-silent scores you will then transmute into living tones. As for compositions that you will buy as you progress and expand, your local music store stands ready to help you. G. Schirmer, Inc., of 3 East 43rd Street, New York City, can supply, over the counter or by mail, almost every piano composition in print, in the Schirmer edition or that of some other firm.

**One copy of Schirmer's excellent "Pocket Manual of Musical Terms" (25¢).**

**One metronome, optional.** Josef Hofmann does not approve of the use of a metronome. He once wrote in answer to a question on this point: "You should not play with the metronome for any length of time, for it lames the musical pulse and kills the vital expression in your playing. Tempo is so intimately related to touch and dynamics that it is in a large measure an individual matter. Consult your own feeling for what is musically right in deciding upon the speed of a piece." Schirmer's *Manual of Musical Terms*, mentioned above, gives definitions of tempo and dynamic directions in all the languages in which you are likely to find them. As for the use of a metronome in beating out time, as apart from its function in setting pace, counting (aloud or to yourself) will serve just as well.

**One system of habits.** To be developed through utilizing the many good ones you have already, altering certain others for our purposes, and adding a few.

— *28* —

## 2

# The Pleasant Necessity
# of Practicing

HABIT is a miraculous thing. To me it is more miraculous than radium or sulfanilamide. From now on we are going to be working closely with Habit, piano playing being a complex of mental and physical habits. Therefore it behooves us to form right habits all along the line, and, having formed them, to make them so intensely ours that they function unconsciously. When you substitute a good habit for a bad one, or when you decide to acquire a habit where none existed before, the new habit must function at first, for a little while, from power supplied by you. This is the stage where we have to make a strong conscious effort, even to the extent of a sensation of spiritual pain. But in a surprisingly short time the habit begins to take over the task of supplying power; it begins to develop its own momentum; and finally we get a sensation of spiritual pain if we *don't* exercise the habit. Furthermore, the period during which a habit functions under its own power is infinitely longer than the initial period when it must function under your consciously supplied power. Hamlet, reasoning with his mother on the topic of dropping a bad habit and substituting a good one, said: "For use almost can change the stamp of nature." As far as piano playing is concerned, I take the liberty of differing with the Bard; I maintain that the word "almost" could be omitted. In this work of improving our piano playing which we have undertaken, there is no more exciting and satisfying phase than that of substituting good habits for bad ones and creating brand-new good ones. Every day of our life, from now on, we will see proof that Habit is miraculous.

The first habit we are going to form is that of daily regularity in our practicing.

The second is that of attacking all our work the hard way, rather than the easy way. This will apply to our mastering of passages in pieces and then to our mastering of entire pieces. We will worm our way, expending considerable effort, into the small end of the cornucopia, in order that we may later emerge, expending less effort and having the time of our life, out of the large end.

Your daily hour should be broken up into three sections—Repertoire, Technique, and Sight Reading. And for the amateur bent on improving his playing in all departments, the greatest of these is Repertoire.

How to subdivide is purely your personal concern. I have split my hour in many different ways; currently I split it as follows:

| | |
|---|---|
| Repertoire | 40 minutes |
| Technique | 10 minutes |
| Sight Reading | 10 minutes |

Perhaps in the early months of this work you may feel it would be wise to work vigorously on your technique, to bring it to, or beyond, its former level when it was at its peak. Such a decision has my hearty approval: obviously, the more technique you have the better. In the chapter on Technique you will find many suggestions. If you make this decision, your hour might be broken up thus:

| | |
|---|---|
| Repertoire | 30 minutes |
| Technique | 20 minutes |
| Sight Reading | 10 minutes |

There are other possible combinations, of course. I suggest that you experiment until you find the one best suited to your needs and inclination. Once you have found it, stick to it only as long as it seems the most efficient one for you. Don't hesitate to revise it as often as the progress of your work dictates.

You will be working according to a schedule, though you will not be a slave to it. You will need a timer. A clock will do. I suggest that you buy an inexpensive clock, christen it your Practicing Clock, and use it for that purpose alone, putting up a terrific fight if one of your loved ones tries to divert it to another use. The "Sessions Timer" has advantages over a clock in that it can be set to measure off any segment of time from five minutes to an hour, ringing a bell to let you know your stint is done. It costs $3.10, comes in a variety of finishes, and is manufactured by the Sessions Clock Company of Forestville, Conn., from whom you can buy it direct. The "Sessions Timer" was designed for use in the kitchen; but if it can efficiently supervise the production of well-done meat loaf, why shouldn't it supervise the production of well-done piano playing? I discontinued its use only because, finding that I could get a half-hour glass ($3) and a ten-minute glass ($1.50), I was quite unable to resist switching over to these charming old-fashioned timekeepers. They have an added advantage: you can lay them flat if the phone rings or the Fuller Brush man calls, and, after the interruption is over, you can set them up and continue without losing a grain of time. But hour glasses and less-than-hour glasses are hard to get just now, being products of France—or what we used to think of as France. I know of only two New York stores which have them today: E. B. Meyrowitz of 520 Fifth Avenue and Parker & Battersby of 30 Rockefeller Plaza.

I think the ten minutes of sight reading could well be left unchanged, no matter how the other two components shift. You shouldn't do less than ten minutes of sight reading a day, but you needn't do more. The more you expand your playing the more you will want to accompany singers and instrumentalists and the more you will want to play in chamber-music groups (see Appendix C); this will provide sight-reading opportunities galore. You can count the first ten minutes of each such session as your day's stint of sight reading, the rest being, as the saying goes, gravy.

If these subdivisions of an hour seem to dwindle into rather short segments of time, I ask you please to bear in mind that we are thinking in terms of years, not days. Bear in mind that 30 minutes of Repertoire a day become 10,950 minutes, or 182 hours, in a year; 910 hours in five years; and 1820 hours in ten years. 20 daily minutes of Technique become 121 hours in a year, 605 hours in five years, and 1210 hours in ten. 10 daily minutes of Sight Reading become 60 hours in a year, 300 in five, 600 in ten. Teresa Carreño's father made her practice sight reading for ten minutes a day—no more and no less—when she was a tot. "And what was the result?"

said the great pianist fifty years later. "By the time I was fourteen I could read anything, absolutely anything, at sight." "Ah," you say, "but that was Carreño." "Ah," I say, "but it is a skeleton in the closet of many a great pianist that he sight-reads poorly. And I personally know one internationally celebrated pianist who can't sight-read for sour apples!"

Practicing, whether of Sight Reading, Technique, or Repertoire, is a pleasure when one is in good spirits. And it goes much deeper than pleasure when one is in low spirits, for it occupies the mind and forces worries into the background; it gives one a tonic sense of achievement; and it often lifts the bad mood entirely. Countless times I have ended in good spirits a practice session that I began in low spirits. "In music," wrote Carreño, "as in all work passionately, devotedly pursued, there is a comfort like the touch of angels' wings. That I need to tell least of all to those who labor lovingly at music, for, of all things in the world to bless us, music stands pre-eminent as solace."

And now, before we begin our long, pleasant task, which we will perform seated at the keyboard of our piano, we ought to get clear on one point. Mark Hambourg's book *How to Play the Piano* contains a wealth of useful material for the earnest amateur; I have already quoted from this book and shall do so again. But when, under the heading, "Position at the Keyboard," he writes that one "should be seated at a medium distance from the keyboard, that is to say neither too near nor too far," I think he is not sufficiently specific. I read this passage the other evening to my friend, George Price, and he agreed that it required elucidation. Turn the page.

*Too Near*

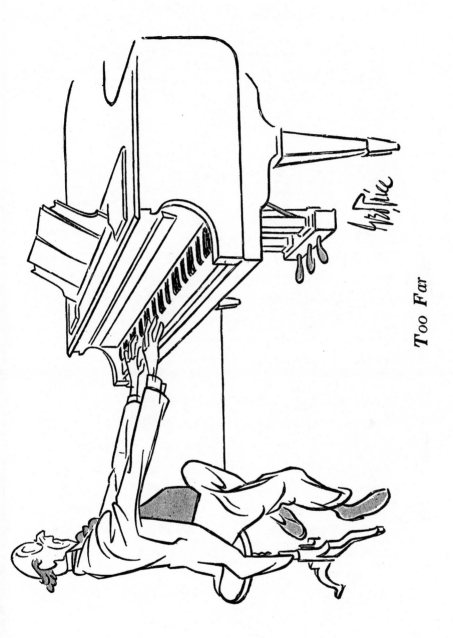

*Too Far*

## 3

# Repertoire

HOBBYISTS, notoriously, are collectors. There are fanatical collectors of stamps, jewels, paintings, antiques, clocks, matchbox covers, Currier & Ives prints, odd-shaped bottles, autographs, entries in a bankbook, and gold ormolu prism chandeliers. The hoarding instinct is as strong in humans as in squirrels, and not confined to the fall of the year.

Hobby pianists are no exception. In fact—I'm going to be snobbish now—they are collectors of one of the least perishable of all commodities. Good music will not merely outlive the paper on which it is written; it will outlive the oils of Raphael, the frescoes of Michelangelo, the sculpture of Praxiteles or even of Epstein. Good music is immortal. Amateur pianists have an advantage over professionals in that they collect for the sheer, uncomplicated love of collecting. And they have an enormous advantage over other collectors: they participate every time they enjoy their collections; they must—

themselves personally—bring alive their various priceless exhibits.

We love and respect our friends each in a different way because each friend is different from every other. Every musical composition we collect becomes our friend—while we are thinking about learning it, while we are learning it, and transcendently after it is learned. It differs from every other composition as humans differ from each other. Like our human friends, it is a warmth in our heart. As with our human friends, we love it more in proportion to the intimacy with which we know it. As with our human friends, the closer we draw to it the more we find in it of value and to value.

*a.*

## Suggestions for your repertoire

Here is a list of twenty-five compositions, all of which are what Bachaus called the "exquisite flowers" of music. They range, technically, from "easy" to "intermediate" and they are tabulated in groups of five. Each group is somewhat more advanced than the preceding one. They may be worked on in any regroupings that might appeal to you—in twos, threes, tens, or as a unit, finally, of twenty-five. And of course out of your previous repertoire and your general knowledge of piano literature you may want to make many substitutions. Above all things, I want you to select for study only pieces that you *want* to play. These, then, I submit as material for the amateur pianist to consider:

Bach—Prelude in C, No. 1 in *The Well-Tempered Clavichord*
Beethoven—Minuet in G
Chopin—Prelude in A, Op. 28, No. 7
Grieg—Nocturne in C, Op. 54, No. 4
MacDowell—*To a Wild Rose*

Bach—Two-Part Invention No. 1
Chopin—Mazurka in A minor, Op. 68, No. 2
Chopin—Prelude in E minor, Op. 28, No. 3
Navarro—*Spanish Dance* (often played as an encore by Jose Iturbi)
Cyril Scott—*Lento*

Bach—Two-Part Invention No. 13
Beethoven—*Album Leaf, "For Elise"*
Godowsky—*Alt Wien*
Granados—*Playera*
Mendelssohn—*Consolation* (*Song Without Words* No. 9)

Chopin—Etude in A flat (posthumous)
Chopin—Prelude in B minor, Op. 28, No. 6
Chopin—Prelude in D flat, Op. 28, No. 15

Mendelssohn—*Confidence* (*Song Without Words* No. 4)

Schumann—*Warum?*

Chopin—Nocturne in E minor, Op. 72, No. 1
Debussy—*La Fille aux cheveux de lin*
Liszt—*Consolation* No. 3
Palmgren—*May Night*
Schumann—*The Prophet Bird*

It occurred to me that you might get further ideas for your repertoire from my own "Group 1" of twenty-five pieces, which I finished memorizing in July, 1938, and now continue to work on, on the easier plane of retention. This group contains some of those listed above, and others:

1. Albeniz—Malagueña
2. Bach—Gavotte and Musette in G minor
3. Bach—Gigue from the B-flat Partita
4. Bach—Two-Part Invention No. 8
5. Brahms—Intermezzo in C, Op. 119, No. 3
6. Brahms—Rhapsody in G minor
7. Chopin—Etude in C minor, Op. 25
8. Chopin—Mazurka in A minor, Op. 68, No. 2
9. Chopin—Waltz in E minor
10. Debussy—*Clair de lune*
11. Debussy—*La Fille aux cheveux de lin*
12. Debussy—*Minstrels*

13. Grieg—Nocturne in C, Op. 54, No. 4
14. Ibert—*The Little White Donkey*
15. Liszt—*Consolation* No. 3
16. Mendelssohn—Scherzo in E minor
17. Navarro—*Spanish Dance*
18. Palmgren—*May Night*
19. Poulenc—*Perpetual Motion*
20. Schumann—*Arabeske*
21. Schumann—*Des Abends*
22. Schumann—*The Prophet Bird*
23. Schumann—*Warum?*
24. Cyril Scott—*Lotus Land*
25. Cyril Scott—*Valse Caprice*

I'm sure it will interest those of you who have read thus far to hear that by practicing according to the methods outlined in this book—by practicing what I preach, in other words—I can "bring back" any one of the above compositions to my finger tips in six repetitions. And I can review the entire group of twenty-five in this way in eight days, giving it three thorough overhaulings in twenty-four days, or considerably less than a month. This is done by—but I'm getting ahead of myself.

At the risk of overstressing the personal note in this book, I am going to list also my "Group II" which, as these pages go to press, I am memorizing. I have been working hard on "Group II" for a long time, and I won't venture a guess as to when I'll have it memorized and can begin retaining:

26. Bach-Busoni—Choral Prelude *I Call on Thee, Lord*
27. Bach-Busoni—Fantasie, C minor
28. Bach-Hess—Choral Prelude *Jesu, Joy of Man's Desiring*
29. Beethoven—Variations in C minor
30. Brahms—Intermezzo, B-flat minor
31. Brahms—Intermezzo in E
32. Chopin—*Berceuse*
33. Chopin—*Écossaises*
34. Chopin—Mazurka in A minor, Op. 41, No. 2
35. Chopin—Nocturne, F sharp
36. Chopin—Prelude Op. 45
37. Chopin—Scherzo, B minor
38. Chopin—Scherzo, B-flat minor
39. Chopin—Waltz in C-sharp minor
40. Chopin-Liszt—*Chant polonais (Moja pieszczotka)* *
41. Debussy—*Cathédrale engloutie*
42. Debussy—*Danseuses de Delphes*
43. Debussy—Prelude (from the suite *Pour le piano*)
44. Debussy—*Reflets dans l'eau*

* Don't let this scare you off. It is translated as *My Joys*, a song Chopin wrote and Liszt transcribed. It is a beautiful composition. Working on it is one of my greatest pieszczotka.

45. Griffes—*The White Peacock*
46. Handel—*The Harmonious Blacksmith*
47. Mozart—Sonata in F (Köchel listing 300K)
48. Rachmaninoff—Prelude in G
49. Schubert-Liszt—*Valse Caprice* No. 6
50. Scriabin—*Flammes sombres*

Recently I memorized, more or less by accident, a delightful antique Spanish sonata by Mateo Albeniz (1760–1831). Now I am confronted by the necessity of deciding which composition to omit from my second group to make room for it. Such a situation is the quintessence of a hobbyist's bliss!

I have set myself a goal of 125 pieces—five groups of twenty-five. When, if ever, I'll attain this goal is problematical. Regardless of final results, however, it is profoundly satisfying to me to know that I have mapped out decades of absorbing hobby work.

### b.
## Transforming weakest passages into strongest

Surgeons tell us that a broken arm or leg, if it is correctly set, becomes strongest at the point of the fracture.

I like to imagine an analogy between this and the process I am about to describe, a process that is fundamental in the task we have set ourselves.

Recognition of the value of working especially hard on difficult passages is no new idea in piano teaching: it is one of the oldest and soundest ideas. But my approach to this factor in piano study is perhaps unique. For I don't approach it with emphasis, or stress, or insistence. I approach it with fanaticism, with mania!

I am now looking you straight in the eye and I am speaking slowly and rather loudly:

I believe in marking off, in every piece we study, all passages that we find especially difficult, and then practicing these passages patiently, concentratedly, intelligently, relentlessly—until we have battered them down, knocked them out, surmounted them, dominated them, conquered them—until we have transformed them, thoroughly and permanently, from the weakest into the strongest passages in the piece.

The cat is now out of the bag. My major premise is stated. I have made a sketch of the foundation on which you can build your piano playing into a structure of dimensions you had thought impossible. Piano teachers in general pay as little attention to this melodramatically sensible approach as they do to having their pupils finish the pieces they start, or retain the pieces they have memorized. Yet this approach has so many shining advantages that I hardly know where to begin in enumerating them.

*Firstly*, transforming a piece's weakest passages into its strongest radically reduces the sum-total difficulty of the piece. Under your gratified eyes, it turns a "Grade VII" piece into·a "Grade II" piece, a "Difficult" piece into an "Intermediate" piece—whatever terminology you want to use.

*Secondly*, each passage isolated for this fanatical treatment illustrates, on a smaller scale, most of the factors that will go into the final process of memorizing the entire piece.

*Thirdly*, each passage thus mastered becomes a fine technical exercise for you: they are all passages which you work on because you find them difficult: you master them for the musical goal of progress toward mastering the entire piece in which they occur: but simultaneously you master the technical problems which make the passages difficult. Thus, as your repertoire steadily expands by means of this system, your technique steadily improves.

*Fourthly*, if you have never memorized music before, this will provide an ideal introduction to a process which you are going to find endlessly interesting. No difficult passage can be mastered without, early in the operation, memorizing it. But passages are not as long as pieces. Passages are a matter of measures, not pages. You can grasp a passage to be conquered with less mental effort than you will have to expend in grasping an entire piece. If you ever do find yourself marking off a fracture which runs to pages rather than measures, the probability is that the piece as a whole is beyond your ability and should be laid aside to take up later.

*Fifthly*, each passage you conquer will give you a sense of achievement which I won't try to describe. You will also get a sense of security, heightened by the knowledge that by your own carefully planned and efficient labor you have leveled to the ground what was a peak of difficulty.

*Sixthly and lastly*, through the faithful use of this method, the next stage in our work—that of memorizing a piece of music in its entirety—becomes so much easier that it is a joy which can well be described as unholy.

You can see that in order to make our later work easier we are indeed going at our present work the hard way, as I said we would. But mark you: conquering difficult passages, though hard, is not forbiddingly hard. Technically we have more to accomplish, but there is the compensation of brevity.

Poldi Mildner planted all this in my brain. Shortly after the sensational debut of this young Austrian pianist in Town Hall in 1932, I asked her how she practiced. I asked her specifically how she practiced Balakirev's tremendously difficult *Islamey*, which she had tossed off like a Beethoven *Bagatelle*. Her answer was brief but illuminating: "I learn first the hard parts, ja." Now we amateurs would consider Balakirev's finger-breaker *all* hard parts, ja. But that needn't stand in the way of our applying Fräulein Mildner's canny advice to music in the wider reaches of the less difficult which we have marked off as our field. In fact, if you work according to my suggestions you will be following Poldi's advice more intensively (as I learned from further conversation with her) than she herself followed it.

I suggest these steps:

Place on your piano rack the score of a piece you have decided to learn or relearn.

Play the piece straight through from the notes, forcing yourself as best you may through any passages of unusual difficulty. This will give you a valuable total impression of the piece and a rough idea of where its "fractures" are. Every place in the piece where you stop or falter is, in greater or less degree, a fracture—a compound or a simple fracture.

Now play the piece through again, halting at every fracture to mark it with your pencil.

This marking is to be done in a special way. Your close attention, please. Include in the fracture a few apropos notes that precede it and a few apropos notes that follow it. To run amuck on figures of speech for a moment, these preceding and following notes are the dowel pins with which you will finally fit the set fracture into its context, like the neat piece of carpenter work it will be. It is essential, for reasons of associative memory, that you always whittle your dowel pins as neatly as you set your fractures.

The actual mark you use may be a cross, a check, a circle, a pointing finger—any mark under the sun except the swastika. I personally mark the beginning thus: ⌈ I place this small mark above the treble staff. I mark the end thus: ⌋ I place it under the bass staff.

These marks should be made firmly enough to be easily seen, but lightly enough to be easily erased when the great moment comes when you are able to tell yourself honestly that what was once a fracture is now one of the strongest passages in the piece.

Our typical fracture is only marked; we must begin setting it:

*Play the passage through slowly several times, always including its dowel pins—making sure that you are reading all the notes correctly, especially the accidentals; making sure that all relative time values of the notes are correct according to the scale of slow motion at which you are playing; making sure that you are following correctly all the dynamic directions (*P, F, SF,

CRESCENDOS, *etc.) and such touch directions (*STACCATO *and* LEGATO*) as there are.*

Be especially careful to choose the fingering which best suits your hand and the phrasing of the passage. Good editions of music usually have sensible fingerings, but if there is any department of piano playing where you should follow your own judgment, it is that of fingering. The best teachers will always tell you that. Even such fine editing as that of Rafael Joseffy should not be followed in its fingering unless you feel that it suits you. In fact Joseffy had some strange fingering crotchets— such as changing fingers on repeated notes even in *molto adagio* passages—which few wish to follow. Try over every fingering that occurs to you and choose the one you want; write it in wherever you need to, lest you forget. Then stick to it. Sometimes, of course, repetition practice itself will show up a weakness of fingering even after you have carefully fingered a passage. In such cases, you should immediately make the change; and I recommend putting a little circle around it, to remind you not to backslide into the fingering you chose first.

**As soon as you are sure of your ground on all these points, play the passage over and over until you have mastered it.**

Tobias Matthay always warned his pupils to beware of "lazy, automatic repetition of passages without thought or meaning, totally lacking in that concentration without which nothing can ever be learned or understood." He called such practicing an attempt to teach a passage *to the piano*, rather than to oneself!

We are going to take Matthay's warning deeply to heart. Our entire mind is going to participate in every repetition of a passage. As a result, this is never going to be dull work: it is going to be lively and absorbing to the $n$th degree.

Predominantly, we are going to practice slowly when setting fractures. "Slow practice is undoubtedly the basis for quick playing" (Josef Hofmann). "Let me recommend very slow playing, with the most minute attention to detail" (Teresa Carreño). "Slow practice does not guarantee concentration, but concentration—especially on problems to be solved—necessitates slow playing" (Egon Petri). "The worst possible thing is to start practicing too fast: it invariably leads to bad results and lengthy delays" (Ernest Schelling).

Even in *prestissimo* passages, piano playing is a series of individual movements fluidly running together. Slow practice enables us to grasp, mentally digest, and physically execute each individual movement that goes to make up the whole.

Work from the notes until you no longer need to. You will find that you soon memorize a passage without having consciously tried to. I don't recommend, at this stage, the use of the many memory aids that I'll discuss in the next section. However, once you have got in the way of searching for, and finding, memory aids in your work on pieces, you will naturally apply this occasionally to fractures. But repetition itself quickly memorizes fractures. After a fracture is memorized, continue to keep the notes in front of you for a while, so that if your memory does play you a trick you can put yourself straight with a glance. Finally, dispense with the notes altogether, drop your eyes permanently to the keyboard, and settle down to setting that fracture.

"Never play a passage twice" (Leschetizky). That's a strange sentiment to place here, isn't it?—and from such an unimpeachable source! Let the great teacher's further words explain his meaning: "Play the passage, then stop and listen to it over again in your mind without playing, then play it again." Because we amateurs are not possessed of the technical ability of Leschetizky pupils, we will have to work harder at the technical side of mastering passages; therefore, I am going to suggest a modification: "Play the passage five times; then stop and listen to it over again in your mind without playing; then play it five more times."

I suggest that you insert frequent repetitions with the eyes closed. Katherine Ruth Heyman insists on this as regular routine in the practicing of all her pupils. It is an integral part of her own practicing when she is preparing a recital program or a concerto. "Inner vision has a far sharper focus than outer vision," she says. If you have never tried this, you will soon see how true it is. Be sure, however, that your concentration is at maximum strength when you practice with your eyes closed.

I suggest that you follow another of Miss Heyman's useful recommendations: when the left-hand part of a passage is more difficult than the right, frequently insert a repetition in which the left hand "leads." That is, play the left hand vigorously and strongly, mentally concentrating on it the while, relegating the right hand to a shadowy *pianissimo*. This is not easy; it takes practice; and it works wonders. Occasionally, for reversed reasons, let the right hand "lead." This is a method more often applicable to the left hand, of course.

I suggest inserting frequent repetitions in which you substitute, for the passage's correct dynamic gradations, a solid dynamic color: *pianissimo; mezzo-forte;* occasionally, when you are sure the neighbors are out, *fortissimo*. Shura Cherkassky, beginning his repetition practice of a passage, usually starts with a *pianissimo* so ghostly soft that it is almost inaudible.

I suggest that you frequently play the right hand and left hand separately. Sometimes many repetitions of one hand alone are useful. Playing one hand alone is *always* revealing.

There are two schools of thought about the tempi of repetition practice. One recommends playing a difficult passage many times very slowly, then testing your progress with a repetition "up to tempo," then many times very slowly again, and so on. It is the method I use and the one I recommend: I make the flat statement that slow practice brings magical results. But you may find that the other way is better for you—that of starting very slowly and, by degrees, increasing your tempo until you reach the indicated speed of the passage. By all means use this method if it brings you better results. Perhaps one method will work for one type of fracture, the other for another. Judge for yourself.

No matter which method you use, here is a useful dodge for especially knotty passages. Get in the habit of frequent repetitions much faster than "up to tempo." When you have so mastered the passage that you can play it well at too-fast speeds, it will be very easy to play it merely "up to tempo" when you place it in its context. This also gives a strong sense of security. I recommend it highly.

Finally, play both hands exactly together when the notes are written to be played together. The fact that Paderewski didn't is no justification. It is a wrong habit,

Paderewski or no Paderewski. Resist the temptation! You may feel sure that you always do play both hands together; even so, it is a good idea to ask a friend to listen to your playing occasionally and check you on this point. Better yet, make a recording of one of your pieces on a home recording machine, if you find one of these instruments in the same room with a piano. You may get the surprise of your life when you play the record back: you may find that your two hands are far less accurately co-ordinated than you thought. The remedy? *Think* both hands together and they'll play together. Get in the habit, too, of listening more carefully to this phase of your playing than you used to.

You may have noted that I have said nothing about the number of repetitions you should play of fractures. That's intentional. It is a matter you can best decide for yourself; doubtless it will never be the same for any two fractures. Twenty-five repetitions is my average daily work on a fracture; to do more would extend my practice time too much. The only generalization that can be made is this: setting a fracture requires *many* daily repetitions (whether ten, twenty-five, or fifty) over an extended period (whether days, weeks, or even, in particularly stubborn cases, months). Our work being hobby work stretching out into years and decades, there is no need to attempt setting any fracture—unless it is the slightest of slight ones—in a day. Just keep at them until they are set.

The question of daily repetitions brings us to the question of whether or not you should use counters. I recommend counters, use them daily, and would not attempt to work without them. But it's another of those things you can best decide for yourself. Some people, while approving the principle of repetition practice, disapprove of counters, on the ground that one's goal should be to practice a passage or piece until one can play it, rather than to achieve a certain number of repetitions. Well, my goal is always to practice a passage or a piece until I can play it, but I have found that the use of counters stimulates me to longer, more efficient, and more thorough work. This may be akin to the fact that dogs race better when paced by a mechanical rabbit. If you do decide to use counters, anything you have at hand will do: matches, slips of paper, checker men. I use a devilishly clever contrivance: the markers from a child's slate, twenty beads strung on two metal rods. It is simplicity itself to flick a bead over after a repetition. This counter system cost one dime. I bought the slate at Woolworth's and sawed off the part I needed.

I suggest that you begin your daily allotment of "Repertoire" time with repetition practice of the fractures you are currently setting. I am always working on two or three fractures in various pieces. I begin each day's practice stint with my multiple setting work; each day the fractures grow stronger; and as soon as one is set, and ready to be fitted into its proper place, I add a new one from my waiting list of fractures which stretches from here to the southern tip of Staten Island. Work steadily and doggedly at your fractures until you can take the splints off them and glory in their strength and certainty and ease of functioning. To me there is no moment more satisfying in piano study than the moment when I know I have completed the setting of a fracture.

Here are some examples of typical fractures (the small-sized notes are the dowel pins). In every case, these fractures are two to several "grades" more difficult than the rest of the piece in which they occur. Examining them will help you in marking off fractures in your own work. I have fingered them with care; but you should follow the indicated fingering only where it suits your hand and your taste. If you have no intention of taking up these pieces, don't put in much time looking over the examples. Study them briefly and move on to the next section, which begins on page 69. If, on the other hand, these pieces interest you, if you would like to play them, try over these fractures on your piano. If you can play them now, you can, with ease, play the pieces in which they occur. If not, try the first steps of setting one of them according to the method just outlined. Judge whether it is a fracture which, by steady and concentrated work, you can set. If it is, you can ultimately play, with ease, the piece in which it occurs.

*From Bach's Gavotte ond Musette in G minor*
*(Allegro con spirito):*

The above fracture and the one that follows are examples of difficulty only slightly greater than the rest of the piece in which they occur. The first one presents the problem of a light, staccato, rhythmic right hand played as accompaniment for a stronger, individually phrased theme in the left hand. Treble and bass must be struck together with the greatest precision, but the timbre and phrasing of the two hands must be contrastingly different. The knottiest spot is the second beat in the third measure: you might make the third measure a fracture-within-a-fracture and practice it twice (until you set it) for every time you practice the whole fracture once. Note that taking the third measure complete provides neat dowel pins for the little fracture-within-a-fracture. As to fingering, the right hand's fourth finger on the opening F may seem strange at first glance; but remember that this is an excerpt from a piece: the fourth finger falls there naturally from the preceding notes. Note how the right hand's fourth begins each group of four eighth notes except one. The trill which is the fracture's concluding dowel pin begins on the auxiliary: B flat.

*From Bach's Gavotte and Musette in G minor:*

The preceding is a passage of repeated notes in the left hand. Von Bülow's (Schirmer edition) fingering for the left hand in the third and fourth measures is 1 1432-1432121. James Friskin recommends 1 21212121231 and I find it easier and better articulated. What fingering suits your hand best here? Experiment a lot before you make your choice.

Now we come to a remarkable pair of fractures. Setting them will make you the possessor of a beautiful Chopin Nocturne which, except in these two places, is

*From Chopin's Nocturne in E minor, Op. 72, No. 1*
*(Andante):*

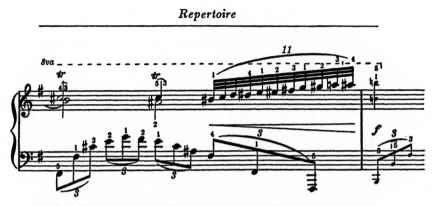

technically simple. These fractures differ from those shown from the Bach Gavotte: they tower above the rest of the composition in difficulty.

In the first, hold the right hand spread wide when you strike the D-sharp grace note; this brings your fifth finger much nearer the F sharp and appreciably increases your chances of striking it accurately. A helpful fingering aid, which you'd doubtless discover for yourself, is to play the E (last right-hand note of the fracture proper) with the thumb and the D sharp-B chord (the right-hand part of the fracture's concluding dowel pin) with $\frac{5}{2}$.

In the second fracture, the problem (apart from the two right-hand runs) is the sustained B (changing to A sharp) under the C-sharp trill. Try various fingerings; Joseffy's is given.

There are four right-hand runs in these two fractures

and the last three of them present problems in poly-rhythm. The first run, being six notes against three, is simple. But this is followed by eight against three, ten against three, and eleven against three. These may be practiced by playing the hands separately and then "putting them together," as many teachers recommend —always thinking ahead to the note or chord on which both hands will "land." Note that in these examples this landing beat is always B—the note B or some form of the chord of B. That is one way to solve these polyrhythmic problems. A second way—more difficult, more interesting, and far more accurate—is to follow the method which Katherine Ruth Heyman uses to solve, with absolute accuracy, all problems in polyrhythm. See Appendix B.

An important general rule for fracture-setting should be applied here: if the work of one hand is easy, begin by learning the easy hand; memorize it quickly, practice it until it is automatic; then you can (almost) forget it as you concentrate, with more of your mind at your disposal, on the other hand's more difficult work. In these fractures the left hand's work is simple, all difficulties being the task of the right hand.

The fracture, on page 61, from Debussy's lovely *Clair de lune*, includes, in the first. full measure, the piece's dynamic climax. Thus it is doubly obligatory for us to set this fracture: weakness of execution can be tolerated least at the moment of climax.

In each of the fracture's two measures, the hands start in contrary motion which changes into parallel motion.

*From Debussy's Clair de lune (Andante très expressif):*

The utmost legato is necessary in both hands. This is made difficult in the left hand by the fact that the notes do not lie well under the fingers. Careful fingering helps in setting this fracture. I have indicated the fingering which, after five years of study and restudy of this composition, has proved most helpful for me. The opening

F sharp in the left hand, a dotted half note, actually is held by the fifth finger only as long as the other notes in the passage are held, e.g., as a legato sixteenth note; making it a dotted half, and tying it to the dotted quarter note on the seventh beat, was Debussy's way of telling us to hold it with the pedal for the entire measure, thus ensuring the typical Debussy "blur" or "cloud" of sound. Note that the concluding F sharp in the second group of six notes in the left hand is played with the fourth finger, but by the fifth in the identical group which follows. The fourth is essential the first time to make the passage flow smoothly. The fifth is taken the second time because the phrasing of the passage at that point permits using this more pianistic fingering; the fifth, used there and again on the immediately following F sharp an octave below, assists the correct phrasing.

If you find that my fingering also suits your hand, take the notes in "handfuls," as the bracket marks indicate. Play each handful ten times—slowly, strongly. Then put the whole left-hand passage together, playing it in the same un-Debussyesque way. Finally add the right hand. Note that the right hand is the same in both measures except for an added voice on the seventh beat of the second full measure. But this added voice makes this the only tricky spot for the right hand in the fracture. Pedaling can, after a fashion, hold the E-G sharp third while the A is added. But shifting the fingers *en-sures* a perfect legato. Shifting from $\frac{3}{1}$ to $\frac{5}{3}$ was difficult for me until I had practiced it a long time. You may not, after a trial, like this. But give it a long trial before you discard it: it has many advantages if you will persevere until it becomes easy.

Finally, of course, the whole passage is to run very smoothly, played in both hands with the "clinging" legato touch required by so much of Debussy's music.

This is a good place to recommend a method of practice which works wonders—I almost wrote "works miracles," so astonishing, quick, and lasting are its results. It was originated by Katherine Ruth Heyman and is called by her the Triple Stroke. To illustrate, I will take the first six left-hand notes of this fracture and rewrite them into a Triple Stroke exercise:

Make one Triple Stroke exercise out of the left-hand passage in the first measure of this fracture; another out of the left-hand passage in the second measure (minus the last five notes, which do not require such intensive treatment). Start slowly, with a cleanly articulated, Mozartean finger stroke; after many slow repetitions, begin to increase the tempo, reducing the height of your finger stroke as your speed increases. In the first slow tempo, accent the large-size notes harshly, softening this, too, as you increase speed. Every tenth repetition or thereabouts, test yourself by playing the left-hand passage as written in the music. You will note remarkable results in a remarkably short time. This method literally brings about triple-riveted finger memory for the passages in which you use it. For another example, if the right-hand runs in the preceding Chopin fractures are difficult for you (aside from their rhythmic problems with the left hand), lift them out of their context and make them into Triple Stroke exercises for the right hand alone until you have conquered them. *Use the Triple Stroke method for all running passage work, right hand or left hand, where you experience difficulty.*

*From Debussy's La Fille aux cheveux de lin (Très calme et doucement expressif):*

This fracture is another in which careful fingering is very helpful. Note that no fingering is shown. You'll enjoy working it out for yourself, and Debussy will beam at you from the other world. He made a great point of not fingering his compositions, and once wrote in this connection: "It is obvious that the same fingering cannot suit differently shaped hands. The absence of fingering provides excellent practice . . . and proves the truth of the old saying: 'One is never better served than by one's self.' "

The single measure from Palmgren's *May Night* on page 66 is our final example of a fracture. It is the only place of any technical difficulty in the piece, and therefore an especially rewarding fracture to work on: set it, and, by following the suggestions on memorizing in the next section, you will soon have an exquisite piece of music in your repertoire. A longer extract from *May Night*, which includes this fracture, illustrates "memory aids" in the next section. If you will cast ahead to this material, which begins on page 84, you will find useful

*From Palmgren's May Night (Poco andante e placido):*

analytical assistance for setting this little fracture.

The next example is not, strictly speaking, a fracture. This opening measure of Chopin's Etude in A flat, Op. 25, No. 1, illustrates something we will occasionally encounter in our piano study. It illustrates a fracture which extends solidly through an entire composition. Master this single measure and you will soon be able to play Chopin's great "Aeolian Harp" Etude, complete. Mastering it is not easy: it means playing the right hand's upper E flats, which come on the beat, with a beautiful singing tone; it means playing the bass A flats, which also come on the beat, firmly but not too loud; it means playing all the inner notes softly and murmurously. When you have done all this, the rest of the composition—if you begin fully relaxed and continue fully relaxed—will give you no trouble, even though the figuration becomes somewhat more elaborate as the piece progresses. The real trick is in that one measure, or for that matter any other measure in the piece except the concluding arpeggios. There are many pieces like this in piano literature.

*From Chopin's Etude in A flat, Op. 25, No. 1*
*(Allegro sostenuto):*

I think I have thoroughly proved my point that fracture setting, far from being dull because it involves repetition, can be the most varied and continuously interesting work imaginable. Mental and manual comprehension of a passage always alters, in repetition practice, according to a gratifying and never-changing progression. First the passage seems strange. Then less strange. Then slightly familiar. Then familiar. Then very familiar. Then you begin to feel a kind of intimacy with it. I think I can best describe the final stage by calling it *deep intimacy*. The passage by that time has become as intimately familiar to you as your own name. I find that the road to this final stage varies with different fractures. Sometimes it is a smooth progression; sometimes more a matter of sudden, unexpected leaps forward. But each repetition—I said *each!*—brings you nearer to the final stage, which Egon Petri has defined as "playing the passage with subconscious, automatic accuracy."

This stage, once achieved, will fade. Further repetition practice will be required to bring it back. With each such fading and retrieving, it becomes still more intimately familiar to you. You will be the best judge of when a fracture is so thoroughly set that it is no longer one of the weakest places in the piece and has become one of the strongest.

Once a fracture is set and placed in its context, you continue to repractice it as you practice memorizing and retaining the piece in which it occurs; thus it continues vividly in your brain and fingers. If you "rest" the piece and take it up again after an interval, the fractures in it will "come back" even more quickly than the body of the piece, because they were more intensively practiced in the first place.

Let us make this mastering of difficult passages a life

habit in our piano study. No other single thing can so smooth the way and lighten the labor of the next stage of our work.

### c.

## Memorizing

We now have on our piano rack the score of a composition which we are going to memorize. The pace of our practicing will change: we will be working on longer lines than those of fracture setting. And this new work will be technically much easier. Mind you, all the fractures in this piece have been set. This has radically reduced the piece's difficulty. And, into the bargain, the once-fractured passages are indelibly memorized—a good start in the process of memorizing the whole piece.

The piece, as I said, is on your piano rack, but I want to digress a moment.

An excellent preliminary step in studying a composition is to hear it played. Get a fellow amateur to play it for you. Hear it played at a recital by a concert pianist. Best of all, buy a record of it. You may not agree with the interpretation of the recording artist—if you don't, so much the better—but hearing the piece will give you a valuable mental picture of it in its entirety. To greater or less degree with different people, having an aural impression of a composition as a whole is an aid to memorizing and interpreting it.

Another preliminary step. Know the piece's key, time signature, tempo indication, and opus number. "Pooh!" you say; "easy!" Pooh? Easy? I suggest a malicious parlor game. Take a Reputable Concert Pianist—any Reputable Concert Pianist. Ask him to name, quickly, one of his Sunday-best pieces. He'll have no difficulty with that. Then ask him to tell you, quickly, what key it is in. His answer probably won't come with reflex rapidity. He will probably say "Er—," blink his eyes, and then give you the correct answer. Now ask him what its time signature is and the fun begins. I have sounded out half a dozen Reputable Concert Pianists in this way and the usual pause is ten seconds—with a few outright inabilities to recall. Now ask your victim, who is getting madder every minute, what the piece's tempo indication is—in the original language and in translation. He may hurl a metronome at you, for it will be ten to one he hasn't the foggiest idea. As to the opus number, he will be certain to know it only if his name is James Friskin. Make it your business to *know* all these things about any piece you are studying. Ingrain these primary facts as thoroughly as you ingrain the composition's notes. Tempo indications in foreign languages should be carefully looked up in your Schirmer's *Pocket Manual of Musical Terms*. Knowing the opus number gives a piece a more intense individuality in your mind; and by doing this with many pieces of any given composer you become able to judge where a composition fits in, in relation to the composer's whole output. Make a game of knowing these facts so thoroughly that you can answer sudden, unexpected questions. Test your certainty by popping the questions yourself. Encourage your wife or husband to ask you; she or he will be only too glad to trip you up if she or he can. Dwell on these points when you're away from the piano—when walking, lying in bed, or sitting bored in a streetcar. It is all very useful knowledge; and it will put you one jump ahead of most concert pianists.

Another preliminary step. Decide on the general character of the piece. Is it meditative, exciting, rhapsodic, martial, humorous, delicate, lyrical, tragic? Is it tempestuous with a middle section of contrasting serenity? Does it tell a definite story, like Brahms' *"Edward" Ballade*? Does it create a certain atmospheric mood, like Debussy's *Clair de lune* or *Reflets dans l'eau*? Does it imitate, like Mendelssohn's *Spinning Song*? Does it mirror in sound a flower (like MacDowell's *To a Wild Rose*) or the flight of a butterfly (like Grieg's *Papillons*)?

The music is still on your piano rack.

Now play the piece through. All the once-difficult passages will flow like oil. Note carefully, without getting up to dance a jig, that where obstacles once stood are now level stretches of mastery. These places are not only conquered technically, but, set here and there in the unmemorized pages, they are oases of perfect memory. Note the resultant increase in your confidence and in your appetite for conquering the entire piece.

*Before you start to memorize it, however, make certain (as you do when you are preparing to set a fracture) that you play all the notes correctly as to identity and time value, that you follow all dynamic and touch directions, and that you choose the fingering which suits you best and write it in where necessary.*

Then get a sense of the form of the piece, that is to say, a sense of its main divisions.

Then carefully note the chord progressions, as apart from the melody line. Note how most "running" passages are built on familiar chords, though at first glance the passage's "passing notes" (notes not from the basic chord) may obscure its fundamental chordal structure. Such passages become instantly less forbidding, and easier to memorize, when we mentally X-ray them and see their bony structure of solid chords. For instance, this superficially complex-seeming passage from Chopin's Etude in C minor, Opus 25, No. 12,

is actually nothing but the chord of C major, without any passing notes. This entire composition can be played through as a series of simple chords, immensely facilitating the process of memorizing it. The following right-hand passage which opens the third movement of Mozart's Sonata in F (Köchel listing 300K) is built entirely on the chord of F major, with passing notes:

Observe how Mozart obligingly lets the left hand state the chord from which he fabricated the ensuing right-hand passage. He does it again, later in the same movement, with the chord of C minor:

Get the habit of playing through the stark skeleton of a composition's basic chords, keeping the mind especially alert as to how the bones are sequentially fitted together. You'll be doing your memory a great service. Furthermore, follow the advice of the master teacher, Tobias Matthay, and always "Think the music from the bass upward." In both basic-chord playing and actual playing, be especially aware of the bass notes—think them clearly and sound them clearly. Be as aware of them as you are of the line of the composition's melodies. "The basses," says Matthay, "must never be thought of as a 'wild grabbing into unknown space' downward from the melody."

James Friskin impresses again and again on his pupils that they should "not only think the music horizontally but listen to it perpendicularly." In the preceding step we have undertaken study of the perpendicular, or chordal, structure of our piece—and we have seen how such analysis helps the memory.

The process of listening to the music horizontally means following the line of the melody. This is such an important factor in piano study that I'm going to speak about it at length, with examples.

First, I suggest that you make a habit of playing through the melody line of an entire piece with the third finger of your right hand. Do this several times. The deeper you impress on your mind the piece's single-note melody line (as though played by an instrument capable of only one note at a time, like the flute) the more that melody line will emerge when you play the piece— which is tantamount to saying the more musical your playing will be.

Following the melody line, and bringing it out in your playing, is not difficult in passages where the melody lies in single notes in the right hand against a left-hand accompaniment. The opening (minus the two introductory left-hand measures) of Liszt's *Consolation* No. 3, on the next page, is a case in point. Your third finger of your right hand will trace this melody line with ease. Having done this, we come to the far more important question of how to play the passage in such a way as to bring out this melody. The passage is marked merely *ppp*. Obviously you cannot follow Liszt's direction that the melody be *cantando* if you play both hands *ppp*. I suggest that you play the left hand *ppp*, the right hand *p*.

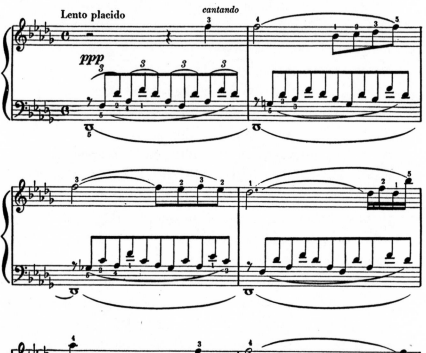

When the melody lies in the left hand against an accompaniment in the right—turn back, for an example, to the first fracture from Bach's G-minor Gavotte on page 56—the task is somewhat more difficult. Not for the tracing third finger of your right hand, but in the actual playing. Here, and in all similar passages, it is very helpful to *think* the melody clearly—this will greatly assist your left hand in bringing it out.

Going on now to the opening of Grieg's lovely little Nocturne (Op. 54, No. 4), page 79, we come to more complex melodic problems. The right hand's first note is in deep bass, its next two in the treble—but all three are part of the main melody line and must stand out accordingly. Note (and play with your right hand's third finger) the left hand's secondary melody: single notes descending chromatically in the first four measures. This, too, must stand out; but only as second fiddle to the right hand in these measures. A very thoughtful adjustment of your dynamic values is required here. In the fifth measure, where the right hand plays two against the left hand's three, observe how Grieg's clever tying of the left-hand notes helps the right-hand melody: no right-hand note is struck *with* any left-hand note. And by playing the grace note before the beat in measures 6 and 8 (instead of on the beat as in music of the classical period), this assistance to the soprano melody is carried right through to measure 13, with the exception of the first beats of measures 9 through 13.

(Parenthetically, may I call your attention to the sequences of circled bass notes in measures 5–9 and 12–13? These illustrate perpendicular musical thinking rather than horizontal. Also, the facts that the first sequence is a four-note chromatic descent, dropping to a D—and the second a two-note whole-tone descent, also dropping to a D—these facts, though mention of them brings us ahead of our story, are Memory Aids.)

Getting back to the horizontal in this fragment of Grieg, note that the right-hand A–A flat in measure 6 and G–F sharp in measure 8 are a subordinate alto melody: don't let it overshadow the soprano melody which, in these measures, is C sharp–D and B–C.

In measures 9 and 11–13, the right hand has the problem of continuing its serene duple-time melody while it also chimes in with the left hand's triple-time accompaniment. This may seem hard at first. It will quickly prove easy, if you isolate measure 5 and practice it as follows: sound the opening right-hand E as though it were not tied; sound all the left-hand notes as though they were not tied; when this measure goes smoothly in two-against-three rhythm (as it soon will), reinsert the ties. Then practice the more complicated measures 9 and 11–13 in the same way.

Going deeper into the subject of melody lines, we come

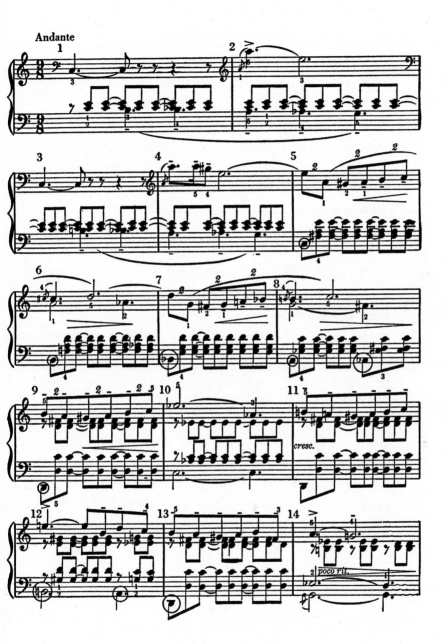

to the very important problem of bringing out melody notes when they are parts of chords. To do this habitually, where the music requires it, is one phase of playing the piano on a higher artistic plane than amateur pianists usually attain to. All artists play this way habitually. A recital by Josef Hofmann is always, among all its other object lessons for the sincere piano student, an object lesson *par excellence* in melody notes sounding, clear and round, out of simple or complex chords of which they are a part.

The excerpt from Chopin's *Berceuse* (opposite) is especially useful for illustration here. Measures 3–6 contain the composition's basic theme in single notes. Don't even bother to play them with your third finger. Note, instead, how with the last beat of measure 6, and on through measure 12, the melody line (slightly varied and extended) is mounted as the top note of two-note chords. Trace *this* melody line with your third finger. This melody must continue, unbroken, the preceding single-note melody, although it now has the competition, in the same hand, of notes which are lower in the scale and consequently heavier in timbre. What to do? Well, a good thing to do is to "lean," slightly but very consciously, on the upper notes, *thinking* them the while more intensely than their accompanying alto notes. Keep at it and soon you will get the effect you want.

With it will come new color and new artistry in your playing. Apply this method to all similar passages in other pieces.

In measure 12 you can go a step further and bring

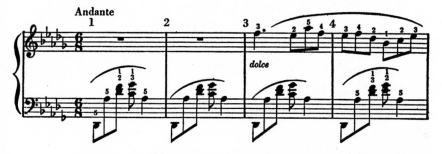

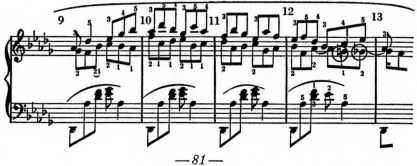

out an *inner* voice: lean here on the alto G and G flat (circled) and you will obtain melodic variety, besides high-lighting a very satisfying modulation and giving yourself practice in still another way to bring out melody notes which are contained in chords. Look for other places in other pieces to apply this: it's a rich field for the imagination and for developing new artistic effects out of the texture of your music. The next time you hear Hofmann play, listen all through the recital for the new, amazing, unexpected beauties of inner voices that he will bring out.

The next-to-closing chord of this same composition provides practice in bringing out a melody note which is part, not of a two-note chord, but of a fat, full chord. Be sure that you bring out the E flat as clearly as the D flat which follows, though the former is in competition with

three other notes in the same hand, the latter with only one. *Lean* on that E flat; *think* that E flat: it will sound for you. Don't forget that this is a *pianissimo*, whispered ending. I suggest *p* for the E flat and D flat, *ppp* for the rest of the notes in both hands. And don't forget to observe the indicated *decrescendo:* make the second $p$ and $ppp$ ever so slightly softer than the first.

**When you are sure of your ground on all these preliminary points—as sure as thoughtful, concentrated study can make you —play the entire composition over and over until you have memorized it.**

Read from the score steadily at first, gradually weaning your eyes away from it altogether. How many days, weeks, or months this will take depends on the composition and on you. Naturally the number of repetitions you do of an entire piece will be much less, per practice session, than those you do of fractures. Each repetition will sink the entire piece deeper into the channels of your memory. I recommend repetition practice of the whole piece, rather than of its parts, because it is technically possible at this stage of our work. And because nothing else gives one such a sense of continuity, such a total "grasp" of the entire piece, and so many valuable supports of associative memory. The peaks of difficulty having been leveled, it all enters the brain and fingers easily.

And remember this: our memorizing faculty is so constituted that it gives the lie to the ordinary laws of matter, for the more memorized music we pack into our brains, the more room there is for still more!

My usual number of daily repetitions of an entire piece is five: two slowly; one up to tempo; two slowly.

We now come to one of the most interesting parts of our work. It is not separate from the repetition practice described above but moves parallel with it. When you have got in the way of looking for, and finding, Memory Aids, every repetition becomes an adventure in discovery.

You will now be finding, every time you play a piece, inner details of similarities, differences, parallels, inversions; all of which will help you in building the upper structure of your memory of the composition.

Mark every one of these detailed Memory Aids on your score.

Don't try to memorize them. Mark them clearly, firmly, and with no expectation of ever erasing them. As you study and restudy compositions through months and years, raising them to higher and higher levels of secure memory, the pages of your scores will become like notebooks in which you have written down more than you can remember. The truth of this will impress itself especially on you when, after thoroughly memorizing a composition in accordance with these suggestions, you drop it for some weeks or months and then pick it up to restudy. Take my word for it, you will then be astonished at, and grateful for, all the Memory Aids you had marked down—and a flock of new Memory Aids will rise up out of the pages, to be in turn noted down with the earlier ones. Notch by notch, your memory of the piece will be jacked up higher and higher. Finally, through this process of repetition memorizing, along with general and detailed analytical memorizing, comes the highest level of memory: intellectual memory. At this level, you will not know a piece because you remember it: *you will remember it because you know it.* At this level, you almost cannot forget a piece if you try. You can "rest" it for a year and, if its technical problems do not require repractice, you can play it almost without a false note. You will be able to "think" the piece through anywhere, anytime—away from the piano or at the piano, at any hour of the day or (unless you're asleep) night. But this is a level we needn't strive for. We will be satisfied with memorizing a piece thoroughly, retaining it indefinitely (see Section *d* following), resting it when we want to, bringing it back when we want to. To attain this lesser but quite sufficient goal, the piece will, through repetition practice, go through the same sequence that fractures (in the process of being set) go through: from strangeness to familiarity to great familiarity to intimacy and finally to deep intimacy. Also, as with fractures, there will be occasional surprising, and gratifying, leaps ahead—often coming just at a time when you had begun to think you were bogging down.

Detailed Memory Aids are enormously helpful; I'm going to convince you of it. Below is a section—measures 20–27—of Palmgren's *May Night:*

And overleaf, my friends, is the same section with the Memory Aids which (to date) I have marked on it.

Those marks weren't drawn on all at once. I have studied and restudied this piece for five years. I purposely chose this passage because it is unusually rich in Memory Aids; richer than most passages. Everything will become clear if you glance at the following tabulation of these Memory Aids. If, however, you are studying *May Night*, don't merely glance at what follows: go over it with a fine-tooth comb:

### General

The passage is dominated by the note B. B is the fifth tone of the scale of the key in which the piece is written: E major. The chord of $B^7$ is the dominant chord of the key of E major.

Embedded in the passage—measures 21 and 22—is the piece's climax. It is a climax of a soft, eloquent phrase (21) and a soft descending passage (22) that moves more swiftly than the rest of the piece. It is not a climax of sound, as in so many pieces. This is a dreamy, haunting composition—a May night to the life in music—and its climax is one of exquisite artistry. The piece as a whole may be described as *dolce;* note, then, how the composer has marked his climax *dolcissimo.*

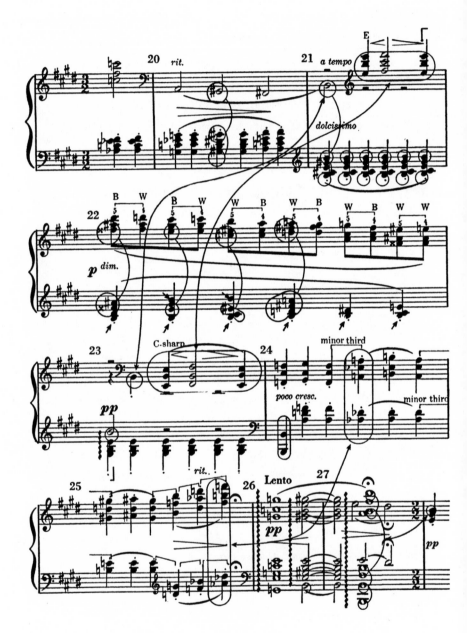

## Measure 20

Contrary motion in the two hands. As the right hand, in deep bass, moves down (a semitone and then a whole tone), the left hand, in middle bass, moves up (two semitones). The center note of the moving voices is identical: G sharp.

Both voices move to B (which, as noted, dominates the passage) on the first beat of measure 21.

## Measure 21

Opens with B in both hands.

B is both the top and bottom note of the left-hand chord throughout the measure.

The first eloquent, but soft, phrase of the climax of the piece occurs in the right hand on the last two beats ( $\frac{3}{2}$ is the time signature here) of this measure. Note, please, that this climactic phrase is, appropriately, the basic musical idea of the entire piece: a chord (quarter note), another chord a whole tone higher (half note), the original chord again (quarter note). See measures 3, 5, 12, 17, 23, 30, and 32 of the composition.

## Measure 22

You may recall from our fracture work (see page 66) that this one measure is the only fracture in the piece. I have marked it here again.

The climactic passage continues and concludes in the

right hand throughout the whole of this measure: a passage of twelve eighth notes. Top line of this passage is a simple chromatic scale descending one octave—from D sharp to E. The passage may also be thought of as broken up into six pairs of eighth notes, each pair fingered 5, 4. I found it also helpful to remember that these pairs are mated thus: black-white; black-white; white-black; white-black; white-black; and white-white.

Note the parallel right-hand and left-hand notes in the first four chords struck together. I found this an especially valuable Memory Aid.

B is the basic note of all six left-hand chords in the measure. B is also the top note of the second and third left-hand chords.

Again, as in measure 20, both hands move toward the note B in the next measure.

### *Measure 23*

The upper, and most important, note of the arpeggiated left-hand chord on the first beat is (you guessed it!) B.

The first note struck by the right hand is B.

Note the parallel between the right-hand passage on the last two beats of this measure and the right-hand passage on the last two beats of measure 21. In this measure, it is a minor tenth lower than in measure 21. In this measure, it differs from measure 21 only in that the middle voice does not move. Note how these chords, in both measures, flower from a deep-bass B taken with the right hand. Note, too, that I have marked the opening chord of this phrase in measure 21 with its highest note, E; that in measure 23 with the corresponding note, C sharp. This is to remind me to *say* these notes when practicing the passage—a device I use very frequently as a Memory Aid in passages that are alike yet unlike.

### *Measure 24*

The octave B is the first chord struck by the left hand.

Right-hand chords now begin a series of statements, differing slightly only as to time value, of the basic musical idea of the piece.

### *Measures 24–25*

This series of right-hand chords ascends in steps of a minor third—the last beat and a half of measure 25 breaking away to ascend one minor third per note instead of per group of three.

Left hand follows a somewhat similar pattern of fourths which ascend in steps of minor thirds. Last three notes of left hand rise similarly to last three of right.

These two measures are written as though in $\frac{2}{2}$ time, with two groups of quarter-note triplets filling each measure, instead of the $\frac{3}{2}$ time in which the bulk of the piece is written.

Note how the complete left-hand and right-hand chord of the fourth quarter note in measure 24 and the final

quarter note in measure 25 are identical—the only difference being the enharmonic one of the way the middle voice
of the right hand is written.

### Measure 26

Second chord is the arpeggio of E major, but based on
the fifth of that key—our familiar B.

### Measure 27

Final chord of the passage is a paradise of Bs. Five of
them, three in the left hand and two in the right. The
chord modulates within itself to a rich, though soft, $B^7$
chord, which is emphasized by being held in a long pause.
And this chord leads on to the next measure, which opens
with a chord of the key of E—a chord of which the top
note is B.

And there you have an example of what I call detailed
Memory Aids. There are half a dozen others in the passage, but they're so slight that I don't consider them
worth the trouble of noting down. I carry them in my
head and, if they slip my mind between restudyings,
they aren't an important loss—other little ones will take
their place. I'm sure you can see that, with all the Memory Aids I have marked down, it would be more difficult
for me, while I'm actively studying *May Night*, to forget this passage than to remember it. And I'm sure you
can also see that if I did not mark them all down, I

would probably forget more than half of them while resting the piece.

Ten years from now I will still be taking up this piece for restudy. And I will still be finding new Memory Aids in the passage we have been examining.


The above space indicates a pause during which author and reader will smoke a cigarette.

All right, here we go again.

The paragraph below is not reprinted by mistake; it is reprinted very much on purpose. Please read it carefully:

"Slow practice is undoubtedly the basis for quick playing" (Josef Hofmann). "Let me recommend very slow playing, with the most minute attention to detail" (Teresa Carreño). "The worst possible thing is to start practicing too fast: it invariably leads to bad results and lengthy delays" (Ernest Schelling).

Slow practice should be used as assiduously for practicing pieces as for setting fractures. You will be amazed, I think, at the rapidity of your progress if you bear this in mind. Josef Hofmann once said in conversation: "Few people realize what can be done by playing a difficult piece six times a day, very slowly, for three weeks; then putting it aside for a few days, and repeating the process."

Shura Cherkassky, once a prodigy of prodigies and now a mature and brilliant artist, might be called, among other things, the world's most accurate pianist. If you agreed to pay a dollar for every wrong note Cherkassky might hit during one of his recitals to a pack-jammed Carnegie Hall, you wouldn't be out of pocket, even if his program included (as it probably would) such oak trees as Balakirev's *Islamey* and the Strauss-Schulz-Evler *Blue Danube* arrangement. All of Shura Cherkassky's preparation is by means of slow— almost agonizingly slow—practice.

I can speak of the value of slow practice from personal experience. I have used it for years and was especially careful to do so in preparation for a short piano recital I played over the National Broadcasting Company's network three years ago. The very words "coast-to-coast network" made my amateur's knuckles knock together and I practiced my pieces as slowly as if the Devil himself sat beside me. The pieces were Grieg's Nocturne in C, Palmgren's *May Night*, and the Schumann *Arabeske*. Well, I didn't play one wrong note—I have a recording of the broadcast to prove it!—and I felt far more freedom for concentration on interpretation than I had thought would be possible under these conditions. My one experience on the radio was for me—and ought to be for all my fellow amateurs—a conclusive, all-time Q.E.D. for slow practice.

You may have been wondering what you should do when, at this point in your work, you play a passage incorrectly. The answer is: don't merely correct the wrong notes and then go on. Go back and choose a dowel pin at the beginning and another at the end of the passage that went wrong; then practice the passage, with its dowel pins, until it runs accurately and smoothly. Otherwise, you will certainly stumble again at the place the next time you come to it. I'm going to make the confident assumption that no such flaw can occur at a place which was originally a fracture; for all the original fractures are of course set and are therefore stronger than any other places in the piece. Consequently, flaws can come only at places which are technically not forbidding. Nevertheless, set them like full-fledged fractures, with all the expertness you have acquired, and fit them snugly into their context. Halting to correct merely the wrong notes themselves will form lamentably wrong associations; it's what Matthay calls, with sublime aptness, Unpractice or Dispractice.

## Touch—the Modern "Weight-Relaxation" Method

Musicologists tell us that Bartolomeo Cristofori, of Florence, built the first true piano—he called it a

"Gravicembalo col Piano e Forte"—in 1708. The entire history of the instrument thus covers a span of about two and a third centuries.

In that time three main types of piano touch have been in vogue. The first—a legacy from the technique of the piano's predecessors, the clavichord and harpsichord—was the finger stroke. It persisted long after the piano had completely superseded its parent instruments. Next came the so-called "pressure touch." This was followed by the "weight-relaxation" touch which for decades has been considered the "right" touch by the best musical minds. Liszt and Rubinstein flourished when the finger-stroke technique, advocated by both Czerny and Clementi, was in fullest flower. Yet we can assume that Liszt must have been relaxed when he played. And we know, from the evidence of Carreño, that Rubinstein was always relaxed in his playing. The Venezuelan pianist, who not only heard many Rubinstein recitals but studied with him, wrote: "Notwithstanding the old rigid school, the great pianists of the past and present have played with great relaxation. Rubinstein is particularly a case in point. He never permitted his body to stiffen when he was at the keyboard. Everything was easy and simple to Rubinstein because he did not try to make a machine of himself."

Carreño's words on the subject of relaxation should

be read with respect and digested with care: in addition to being the greatest of women pianists, she mastered relaxation to a greater degree than any other pianist with the possible exception of Godowsky. Below, combined into one paragraph, are selected thoughts on relaxation expressed by Carreño at different times during her life:

"The great principle in piano playing—relaxation—is what I seek most indefatigably to inculcate in my pupils. By relaxation I do not mean flabbiness or the tendency of some pupils to flop all over the piano. Relaxation signifies control, and it affects the mentality of the pianist no less than his fingers, hands, and arms. The tension under which so many players labor is dreadful. It is seen even in the muscles of the neck and face. Too few pupils can be made to understand that relaxation is achieved through a mental process. It is really mental relaxation: one has to think it. It has to be in the mind first before it can be worked out in the arms, hands, and fingers. We have to think it and then act it. The basis of all playing is sensible relaxation. At the keyboard the body must be in such a state that it will always respond to the commands of the mind. This is best accomplished through controlled relaxation. With a rigid forearm, fingers working like hammers, and a hand bobbing up and down like a butcher's cleaver, the tone colors are so lacking in variety; so hard and unengaging, that it is a marvel to think that such a school of instruction could ever have been in supremacy for so many years. The tone colors are all in the arm—the relaxed arm. Actually, relaxation means to loosen just where needed and nowhere else. The secret of power lies in relaxation; or, I might say, power *is* relaxation. It is through relaxation that I am able to play for hours without the slightest fatigue." *

Carreño has told us about Rubinstein's relaxation; now let Ethel Leginska tell us about Carreño's relaxation:

"Relaxation is a hobby with me," Leginska once said. "I believe in absolute freedom in every part of the arm anatomy, from the shoulder down to the finger tips. Stiffness seems to me the most reprehensible thing in piano playing, as well as the most common fault with all kinds of players. While living in Berlin, I saw much of Mme Carreño, and she feels the same as I do about relaxation—not only at the keyboard, but when sitting, moving about, or walking. She has thought along this line so constantly that sometimes, if carrying something in her hand, she will inadvertently let it drop without realizing it, from sheer force of the habit of relaxation."

Recently all my resolutions to relax when I play were

* These quotations are reprinted, with permission, from the unique and irreplaceable scrapbook of Carreño memorabilia collected by Vincent de Sola.

greatly strengthened. Vincent de Sola, the Cuban-American pianist, showed me a cherished communication from a friend. An excerpt reads: *No se olvide cuando toque piano de aflojar los brazos y las manos.* ("Do not forget when you play the piano to loosen the arms and the hands.") These words were written on November 4, 1916, by Teresa Carreño, eight months before her death.

Tobias Matthay's monumental work, *The Act of Touch in All Its Diversity,* * was published in 1903. It brought about a revolution in piano teaching because it installed weight-relaxation—logically, sensibly, and with microscopic analysis—as the correct method of piano touch. I recommend especially that you read Part III of this work—"Key Treatment from its Muscular Aspect."

Leopold Godowsky was a past master of weight-relaxation. Once he told a friend how he happened to adopt this touch and develop it to such a great degree. Around the turn of the century, Godowsky was practicing twelve to fourteen hours a day. He found that as he neared the end of his exhausting daily task, so fatigued that he could hardly keep his fingers on the keys, his playing got better and better. Being as great an analyst as he was pianist, this paradox piqued his interest.

* Longmans, Green.

He studied and compared all his muscular actions during several of his long practice sessions, and came to the conclusion that it was the dead-weight muscular "drop" of the later hours of his practice sessions that brought about these rich, fluent, and lyrical results. He began to imitate consciously this "drop" at the beginning of a practice session and carry it straight through. The result, gradually perfected, was a transformation of his playing into the method for which he became famous. "In this method of playing," he wrote later, "the fingers are virtually 'glued to the keys' in that they leave them the least possible distance to accomplish their essential aims. This results in no waste motion of any kind, no loss of power, and consequently the greatest possible conservation of energy."

Moral: one way, according to Godowsky, to approximate the condition of weight-relaxation touch is to consciously imitate, from the shoulder to the finger tips, a sense of extreme muscular fatigue.

James Friskin, who studied with Matthay, recommends that his pupils, during practice periods, frequently drop their arms to their sides, dangle them inertly—"like ropes"—then lift them to the keyboard and, maintaining their relaxed condition, resume playing.

Ossip Gabrilowitsch once said: "The full-arm touch,

in which I experience a complete relaxation of the arm from the shoulder to the finger tips, is the condition I employ at most times. You will observe by placing your hand upon my shoulder that even with the movement of the single finger a muscular activity may be detected at the shoulder. This shows how completely relaxed I keep my entire arm. It is only in this way that I can produce the right kind of singing tone in cantabile passages."

Katherine Ruth Heyman's relaxation is so perfect that the movement of a single finger may be detected in the muscles, not merely of her shoulder, but of her back.

If you wish to develop relaxation in your playing, try an experiment. Play a solid chord with both hands, with the touch you are accustomed to using. Now, holding the fingers in place, relax the arms so completely that they would fall to your sides if they were not held up by the keyboard. Now relax *before* you play the same chord: you will note an increase in richness of tone. Try this same sequence with each note of a scale played very slowly. Gradually increase the tempo. Take a passage from one of your pieces—say a fracture you have recently set—and apply this sequence. As a general rule, relax as completely as possible, *sending your consciousness down to your finger tips*.

It is often helpful, if relaxation does not come easily, to leave the piano, lie down, close your eyes, and *think* of yourself playing in a wonderfully, ideally relaxed way. Try this for passages, for whole pieces, and for your playing generally. If you do it many times, the chances are excellent that relaxation will come to you— and remain.

I am indebted to Ian Mininberg, editor of *Keyboard*, the magazine for piano teachers, for a very valuable habit to acquire. I began applying it the first day I heard of it and make increasing use of it all the time. It is not the same as relaxation, but is related to it. Mr. Mininberg suggests going through every piece we are studying and selecting places where we can "rest on the keyboard." At such "resting points" your muscles will get a fresh lease of strength (for even in the most perfectly relaxed playing there is muscular activity) and you will be constantly (to coin a word) re-relaxing. Often one hand can rest while the other continues active playing; often both hands can rest together. I go through all my pieces marking such resting places with a large capital *R*.

### INTERPRETATION

Josef Hofmann has written:

"The artist expresses his feelings with due deference to the canons of art. Above all, he plays correctly. Without unduly repressing his individuality, he respects the composer's intentions by punctiliously obeying every hint or suggestion he finds concerning speed, force, touch, changes, contrasts, and so on. He delivers the composer's message truthfully. Not so the amateur. Long before he is able to play a piece correctly, he begins to twist and turn things in it to suit himself. Feeling is a great thing; so is the will to express it: but both are worthless without ability. Hence, before playing with feeling, it were well to make sure that everything in the piece is in the right place, in the right time, strength, touch, and so forth."

Let us not be discouraged by the master's blunt words. Let us be inspired by them to play, as amateurs, in a way that might win his approval. Let us burn his concluding sentence, above, into our brains; let us make it our creed. Let us never concern ourselves with "interpretation" until we are certain—as certain as it is in our power to be—of the accuracy and fidelity which Dr. Hofmann's ideals demand.

Only then can we begin to enjoy the crowning satisfaction toward which all our work has been leading.

Your interpretation must be built on a foundation as solid as rock: all technical difficulties must have been mastered; memory of the entire piece, its notes and its dynamic markings, must be secure; fidelity to the intended spirit of the piece must be equally secure. Only after he has laid such a massive foundation can the amateur concern himself with interpretation.

What can I say that would be helpful on this topmost level of our work? Very little. Such ideas as I may have been able to give you about piano study do not extend to this level, where, granted the controlling factors already mentioned, you become monarch of all you survey. These are Mark Hambourg's eloquent words on the subject of "Interpretation": "Musical compositions may well be compared to beautiful landscapes, which are constantly changing in color and effect through the action of atmospheric conditions; on no two days does a landscape look exactly alike, yet its composition and outline remain fixed, everlasting." And these are the eloquent words of Teresa Carreño on the same subject: "No matter how often I go over a composition, I see new charm, new delight, new fascination, new poetry in each repetition. What a glorious opportunity for artistic experiment does the practice period become! No interpretation is a good interpretation if it is fixed and immobile. No matter how we might try, it would be impossible ever to play a composition twice alike. There is an enormous area for variation. It is this which gives such infinite charm to piano playing."

Of all the arts, music requires most of the interpreter; he is, in fact, a co-creator. A musical composition, until it is played, is but ink on paper; it does not reach its final fulfillment until the performer, sifting it without distortion through his personality and temperament, brings it alive in the brain of the hearer. Beethoven said: "Music conveys messages from heart to heart." Pepito Arriola, a piano prodigy, once said with wisdom beyond his years: "Music tells things that cannot be told in words." William James, the philosopher, said: "Music is the element through which we are best spoken to by mystical truth." Katherine Ruth Heyman concluded an article entitled "Music: from the Dream to the Dream" with these words: "These, then, are the five stages of the Dream: the Dream in the mind of the composer; the record; the perception of the Dream in the heart of the artist; the presentation; the composer's Dream in the mind of the hearer."

"My only method," Walter Gieseking once said to an interviewer, "is to evolve a clear and complete conception of what I want to do with a piece." May I re-emphasize here the importance of deciding, before you begin to memorize, what the character of a piece is? Then, having decided, think about it when you are not practicing; let it sing in your brain; walk to its rhythms in the street. "Fine playing," says Sergei Rachmaninoff, "requires much deep thought away from the keyboard. The student must not feel that when the notes can be played his task is done: it has only begun." This deep thought may also be practiced at the keyboard while you are making your slow repetitions of a piece, which outnumber your repetitions "up to tempo" by four or five to one. I have found that more ideas for interpretation come to me when I am slowly and carefully practicing a piece than when I am playing it through at its proper speed. Once the fractures of a piece are set, in fact, encourage your mind to ponder your interpretation at every subsequent stage of your preparation of the piece. Listening intently to your playing, as though it were someone else, will give you valuable interpretative ideas. Ferruccio Busoni used to say, "At my recitals no one listens more attentively than I do."

Reading about the composer and (if such material is extant) about the piece itself is helpful. The more rounded out your general musical knowledge is, the richer and more authentic your interpretations will be. In the bibliography at the end of this book you will find a list of books on music in general and piano music in particular.

Next to locating the climax of a piece and building the dimensions of your interpretation with reference to that climax, I think the most important thing about interpretation to remember is this: always strive for a singing tone. The structure of the piano makes it impossible for us to change the quality of a tone after it has been struck, except by pedaling. Our problem is to get the best approximation we can to vocal tone or the tone of an instrument played with a bow. Vladimir Horowitz said recently: "Now, I assure you, the moment I conclude that the piano is nothing but an instrument of percussion, to be beaten or whacked in order to make rhythm or some hard percussive sound, and not as an instrument on which to sing—in that moment I shall lock up the instrument and certainly never play again!" How far you will succeed in making the piano sing is largely up to you. "The sensitiveness of the piano," wrote Ernest Hutcheson, "is, I am convinced, seldom realized. Treat a piano badly and it will sulkily lock up its treasures of tone. Treat it lovingly and understandingly and—with its harp of over two hundred strings, its great sounding board and frame, and its system of pedals—it is one of the most responsive of instruments."

To make the piano sing was always a primary tenet in the teaching of Leschetizky. It was always, naturally, a primary concern of Leschetizky's greatest pupil, Paderewski—and how triumphantly he succeeded! One of the best ways to train yourself in this playing habit is to listen to Paderewski's recordings.

*Think* of the melody line as song: this will help you astonishingly toward making it sound like song. Think of the melody line as a long wordless, properly punctuated song, rather than as a series of tones emanating from hammer-struck strings. This can be done in almost all compositions, but especially in compositions which are predominantly lyrical in character. If you have never before specifically set out to make a piano sing, prepare yourself for a big surprise. I mean the surprise you will get when you realize how amazingly responsive the piano is to such an approach, how much the piano itself loves to sing!

And there is the matter of tonal color, which you should use generously. Excellent counsel is that of Anton Rubinstein, who said to his pupil Felix Blumenfeld, who told it to his pupil Vladimir Horowitz: "Do not try to imitate orchestral instruments on the piano, but think of the colors of these instruments as you play."

It was Horowitz himself, one of the great colorists, who, in an interview in *The Etude*'s issue of March, 1932, made the subject of piano color come alive most vividly for me with one brief paragraph of comment and one brief musical illustration:

"In searching for tone quality," Horowitz said to Florence Leonard, "it is helpful to think of the instruments of the orchestra. I think of many instruments when I play. I do not mean that one should try to imitate, for the timbre of the piano is not the timbre of the violin nor the bassoon nor the flute. But if one thinks of the quality or the sonority of the various instruments, one is helped to play more beautifully. We have, in the piano, all registers—flute, oboe, violin, viola, clarinet, cello, double bass. If, when I play from Beethoven's Sonata Op. 10, No. 3,

I think 'double bass,' then the color is better."

"Color means everything to the pianist" (Carreño).

*Tempo rubato* and pedaling are difficult subjects to discuss usefully in a book. As to the former, once you have grasped a piece's rhythmic structure accurately— *play flexibly.* As one comes forward from Bach through Beethoven to Chopin, flexibility in playing should increase. Be aware of bar lines as marking off the rhythmic segments of a composition: "leaning" almost imperceptibly on the first beat of measures is often of value: it keeps the rhythmic flow going and gives you freedom for flexibility within the remaining beats in the measure. But beware of making a general rule of this. When the phrases of a piece do not conform in shape, or fractions of their shape, to the piece's bar lines, this rule must be modified; sometimes abolished.

As to pedaling, *listening* to your own playing will tell you more than any printed words can.

Surely you are convinced by now that repetition practice can be, and should be, endlessly and increasingly interesting work: from the mechanical side as you memorize; from the spiritual side as you ripen your interpretation. The processes aren't separate, but intimately related: you will never play a composition through slowly, for purposes of memorizing, without also getting interpretative ideas; just as surely, you will never play it through up to tempo without strengthening your memory.

Be critical of your interpretative ideas as they develop. Don't ever adopt one unless you are sure it is sound. Then if a new idea comes along which, on careful thought, seems superior, make the substitution. What should be your criterion? Your own musical taste. Within the limits of fidelity to the letter and spirit of the composer's intentions, your interpretation should be plastic—susceptible to the influences of your mood, the conditions under which you are playing, and the mood of your listeners. If you have no listeners, that creates a mood of its own.

Every time you play a piece you move one step further in the long process which Moriz Rosenthal calls "getting a piece into your fingers and into your heart and nailing it down in your brain."

I want to conclude this section on "Interpretation"

with the words of the Máster of Master Pianists, Franz Liszt:

"The pianist is not a mason who, chisel in hand, faithfully and conscientiously cuts his stone after the design of the architect. He is not a passive tool that reproduces feeling and thought without adding himself. Musical works are in reality only the tragic and touching *mise-en-scène* for feelings; the pianist is called upon to let these speak, weep, sing, sigh. He creates in this way like the composer himself. He breathes life into the music's body, infuses it with gracefulness, charm, and fire."

## *d.*
### After memorizing—retention

Nails, with the passing of time, work loose. But it is far easier to tighten nails that have worked loose than to drive those nails in in the first place: a few expert blows with a hammer and they are firmer than ever. A few expert blows on the incorporeal nails with which we're working and *they* are firmer than ever!

I have a quarrel with most piano teachers. I will try to give you my side. I hope that when I finish, you will see eye to eye with me; I hope that my view will influence your piano study for the rest of your life.

We study the piano in order to play it, do we not? I

grant that browsing and ensemble playing and accompanying are pleasant and soul-satisfying results of piano study. But I feel that playing pieces is indubitably the major and most gratifying goal of study of this essentially solo instrument. You agree? Can you explain to me, then, why piano teachers thoroughly teach fine compositions to their pupils and then complacently let these compositions slip through their pupils' fingers? Or, worse, partially teach fine compositions to their pupils, drop them, and go on to new work before the old work is done?

Of all sad words of tongue or pen, the saddest (and most inexcusable) are these: "I used to play it." Next saddest, and next most inexcusable: "I began it, but I didn't finish it."

It is unfair to the world's piano teachers—an exceptionally intelligent, skilled, and idealistic corps—to place the blame wholly on them. Their pupils are equally at fault: unless they are earnest conservatory students, they are likely to grow restive under the higher discipline of retaining a piece once it is learned. They tend to leave one composition unfinished and skitter over, like a water bug, to another which is more alluring only because it is newer. Their manner of study simply does not include habitual work on the plane of retention, or habitual work on the plane of finishing the

pieces they start. And their teachers concur in this lax-
ness because a restive pupil turns, lamentably often,
into a lost pupil.

I said earlier that we amateur pianists collect fragments of immortal beauty. Let us really collect, then.
Let us make it our compulsive necessity never to "lose"
a piece of music we have once learned. Let us, first, finish
every piece we start. And let us retain every piece we
finish. If a stamp collector loses one of his rare items, he
is likely to smash everything within reach and then go
crazy. Let us borrow the spirit, if not the letter, of this
fanatical acquisitiveness. For what, after all, would you
think of a jewel collector who said: "That blue-white
diamond? Yes, I used to have it. But I've lost it or mis-
laid it. I don't know exactly what happened to it, but it
isn't in my collection any more." You'd think he was a
poor specimen of a collector. Well, if you play Grieg's
Nocturne in C or Chopin's Prelude in A or the Schumann *Arabeske* or any one of hundreds of compositions
of equivalent fineness of fiber, you own a lovely blue-
white diamond. You own it far more completely and intimately than any jewel collector can own a jewel. Lose
it? Mislay it?

I make two exceptions to my blanket demand that we
finish, and retain, every piece we start. Drop, without
regret, any piece that you find is beyond you technically.

Drop, without regret, any piece that you find you honestly dislike. But there's a catch even here. Your technique will be improving all the time and you will, as the years go by, "catch up" with many pieces which were once beyond your powers. And what you thought was honest dislike often turns out to have been just staleness. You will often return to a piece with a fine appetite after a year or five years, absence having made the heart grow fond again.

Let us never say: "I began it, but I didn't finish it." If we apply the methods in the section on "Memorizing," we will have finished it. That done, let us never, *never* say: "I used to play it."

By going at our tasks the hard way, we now come into our greatest reward: retention is easier work than memorizing.

And this is the way it's done:

**To retain pieces you have memorized, simply play them over once or twice during your practice period.**

Naturally, you will be busy all the while with the harder work of setting fractures and memorizing new pieces—the bulk of your "Repertoire" time should go to that. Therefore, don't ever play more than two repetitions, in one day, of a piece you are retaining. Be sure to play it slowly at least once for every time you play it up to tempo. Keep the score within easy reach: leaning on the score for support of an unaccountable lapse of memory in a well-learned piece is like leaning against a solid wall. Leaning on your memory for a lapse of memory often leads to a sense of panic and to a virtual certainty that you will come a cropper at the place the very next time you play the piece. Lastly, don't do retaining work on any single piece on consecutive days. Do it on alternate days, or twice a week, or once a week. No memorized piece, if you work once a week on retaining it, will ever become a piece you "used to play." You will never be sorry if you adopt this new view of piano study: your work will be firmer, solider, more satisfying, more absorbing. Your results will be richer; and they will be *permanent*.

The process of restudying a thoroughly learned piece which you have purposely rested is different. It is more like the original process of learning the piece—but far faster. The fractures often have to be reset, but that, you'll find, will only take a tithe of the time it took when you first did it. Such a sediment of work will have accumulated from your earlier studying or studyings of the piece that the process of "bringing it back" will seem almost magically fast.

I confess that I prefer the harder work of memorizing to that of retention, but that's because I'm a hobbyist of deepest dye who, like his unreasonable brother fanatics in other hobbies, has for his motto: "The more work, the better I like it!"

But there are pleasant freedoms in retention work. The more pieces you memorize, the more you shuffle them around to decide which, on any given day, are to be worked on for retention. You don't inch along as you sometimes have to in memorizing: your stride is longer and more relaxed, even when you are playing a slow repetition. Your concentration is now on the high plane of interpretation: your pencil doesn't fly up to mark a B flat in the treble which, with a hitherto unnoticed parallel of a B flat in the bass, makes a new memory aid. No! Your pencil marks "Eloquently" here, or "A distant echo" there, or a general admonition to yourself: "This piece should be brilliant and stirring, but not bangy."

Each thoughtful retention-repetition will of course tighten any memory nails that have worked loose. And it will do far more. It is the same with the musical compositions we have learned as it is with our friends: the more intimately we know them the more we value them, the more we warm to them, the more we appreciate their depth of character and their worth. Fine music is depthless—do you remember my mentioning that Moriz Rosenthal is still finding deeper levels of beauty in Chopin's

Prelude in A? The interpretative part of our retention work can go on for the rest of our lives.

And now, turning from the spiritual to the practical, let us consider the question of how to organize our musical scores. Until a piece is memorized, it needn't be organized—let it live a nomad's life on your piano rack, piano top, in your piano bench, and under the table where the electric fan blew it. But once it has been memorized, once it has proudly graduated to the status of "To be retained," then it should be organized. Then the collecting instinct, which runs like a leitmotiv through our work, should come right out into the full brasses and assert itself.

Collect your memorized pieces into groups. When you have two, put together these two hard-worked, dog-eared, marked-up, weary but game scores. The same with five, ten, or twenty-five.

I think it's helpful to number your pieces, arranging them alphabetically according to composers; but that's up to you. I also think that the moment of transition to the "To be retained" category is a fine time to repair a score with transparent tape. It will—at any rate it should—need repairing badly, at this point.

I had a special loose-leaf notebook made for my first group of twenty-five. It cost a pretty penny. It has covers of fine-grained leather. It has a place marker of black silk. It is very handsome. It isn't worth a damn. I do not recommend it, any more than I recommend rolling in flypaper. The pages don't turn easily. Most of the time they don't turn at all. The holes I laboriously punched in the music have ripped through. The entire contraption weighs more than a copy of *Anthony Adverse*. In fact, the very next rainy morning, I'm going to take my music out of this monstrosity—which my wife refers to as "Cooke's Folly"—and arrange it as I suggest that you arrange yours: in the Clayton F. Summy Company's "Musifile," * which compactly holds, in classified compartments, up to 200 compositions.

### *e.*
## Playing for others

For a long time war raged between me and two of my most beloved friends. In the best modern manner, it was an undeclared war. And in the best modern manner, it was a bitter struggle to the finish. They won.

The point at issue was simple and clean-cut. My war aim was to play the piano for them, occasionally. Theirs was not to have me play the piano for them, ever. And the war guilt was not theirs. It was mine.

* Clayton F. Summy Company, 19 West 44th Street, New York City. $1.69.

At this point we should face a fact: there is a strong tinge of ego in every hobby. This is as true of piano playing as of any other—perhaps a little more so. Not that this is reprehensible; it is normal and healthy and human—but it shouldn't be allowed to get out of bounds. Candor compels me to confess that in my early years of hobby work at the piano, my attitude, when unsuspecting friends came to call of an evening, was often as follows: "I have just finished learning Debussy's *Clair de lune*. This excites me. Whether it excites you is beside the point. I am now going to play Debussy's *Clair de lune* for you, willy, nilly, hell, or high water." Some friends enjoyed it. Some could take it or leave it. Some could leave it.

Spectacularly first in the last category were the two friends previously mentioned. But the glum silence with which they watched me sit at the piano, and the glummer silence which followed my playing, did not curb my singleness of purpose. Clear as sky-writing in my brain were the words of Leschetizky: "The wise one will gather his friends and also his enemies together, and try to please them. It is necessary to play before people. Make them listen whether they want to or not. Scratch on their doors to be allowed to play. You may think you have a piece learned, but you never know until you have played it before people." Likewise the words of Josef Hofmann: "To play for people is not only a good incentive for further aspirations; it also furnishes you with a fairly exact estimate of your abilities and shortcomings, and indicates thereby the road to improvement. I recommend playing for people moderately, on the condition that for every 'performance' of a piece you play it afterward twice, slowly and carefully. This will keep the piece intact and bring you many other unexpected advantages." Thus armed with august approval, I was not even moved to pity by seeing, as I strode implacably to the piano, the genuine suffering, the spiritual torture, the *Weltschmerz* that clouded my two friends' otherwise affable brows.

This war went on, as I said, for a long time. What brought me to my senses was myself. At the home of some other friends one evening, a young poet with a hitherto innocent record suddenly announced that he had just finished a narrative poem running to sixty pages and would now read it to us. He whipped a plump manuscript out of his pocket and unfolded it. And just at that instant I caught a glimpse of my face in a mirror. I am practically stone-deaf to poetry and my face in the mirror bore the same ghastly evidence of pain that I had often seen on the faces of my two friends.

The poet read on and on. And on and on. And all at once I had a revelation and made a decision: "My friends suffer while I play as I now suffer while he reads. I will never, never subject them to the ordeal again.

Particularly as this Torquemada is a professional poet and I am only an amateur pianist."

And from that day I have never played for anybody who I knew did not want to hear the music I was able to make.

There are, you will find, many music-loving people who enjoy hearing amateurs play—naturally the better the playing is the more these people enjoy it.

I venture this generalization: play, every time you get a chance, for such friends as truly want to hear you. And I also suggest that you sometimes play for such friends of yours who are this way and that about it—who don't care whether you do or don't play. They may find they like it more than they had anticipated.

There are advantages in playing for people which you can gain in no other way. Having an audience radically changes your relation to the piano and to the piece you are playing. This is excellent. Weak places turn up where you had least suspected them. These you should mark as fractures, practice as fractures, and work on until you have set them. You'll find them much easier to set than the piece's original true fractures, for they are pseudo-fractures caused by the healthy nervousness which an audience, even of only one person, produces; or by the unfamiliar feel of the keyboard of a strange piano; or the unaccustomed height of a strange piano stool. All of which is a wonderful tonic for your work. Put all such pseudo-fractures at the head of your current fracture list and set them with all the loving care with which you set true fractures. Gradually you will arrive at the point where you can play your pieces well under almost any conditions.

Playing for others will sometimes cause unexpected, and seemingly inexplicable, lapses of memory. Don't worry if this happens, even if you had to stop dead at the place and finally, in order to finish the piece, take it up from a later point. Be glad that the presence of an audience showed up the insecure spot. The very next day, and on as many successive days as are necessary, practice that spot right into the ground; practice it until it can never halt you again.

When playing for people, relax even before you sit down, and stay relaxed until you finish playing. Think the opening measures of the piece before you raise your hands to the keyboard. Raise your hands unhurriedly and begin unhurriedly. Play a little more slowly than the piece's indicated tempo; this will give you a sense of greater security and will counteract the almost universal tendency to play faster when playing for people. Try to keep your mind entirely on the music and not at all on your hearers.

What about comments on your playing? Encourage them. Encourage critical comments especially. Lesche-tizky said: "We learn much from the disagreeable things people say, for they make us think; whereas the good things only make us glad." Turn to your own constructive ends such critical comments as seem to you, after reflection, to have been justified. And there is but one thing to do with critical comments which, after reflection, seem to you to have been unjustified: forget them. If people praise your work, be pleased—and work hard to do better the next time. The excitement of playing for people is very good for you; if your pieces are thoroughly learned, it will stimulate you to play "better than you know how."

But playing for others is only a by-product of our work. Opportunities for it will crop up now and again. You should do it—to give such pleasure as you can with your music, to discipline yourself, and to discover whether you really know your repertoire as thoroughly as you think you do. But keep to the work: it is a glorious end in itself as it slowly but surely improves your playing and thereby intensifies all your enjoyment of music. The work's the thing!

### *f.*
### "What shall I learn next?"

Once the amateur pianist has his hobby well started, a certain delightful moment recurs periodically in his life.

It is the moment when, having memorized a piece and placed it on his "To be retained" list, he turns to the treasure house of piano literature to select the next piece that he will make his own. He has behind him, at this enviable moment, work well done. He has before him, within reach, no matter what the level of his technical ability, a display of priceless treasures that outdazzles the loot in Ali Baba's cave. He runs his eye over the exhibits which glint like diamonds set in platinum. Excited by his opportunity, he considers long. He will not take this one just now, nor this one. He will take that one. Yes, that is the one he will now add to his precious collection. He will not obtain it with money or by theft. He will buy it with work. And, curiously, after he has made it intimately and permanently his own, it will still be there for other treasure seekers like himself to take. It will always be there. And so will all the other treasures prodigally heaped around it.

Moreover, the amateur pianist, leaving Ali Baba's cave with his new piece of treasure, exults in the knowledge that he will come back later for some of the others.

## 4

# Technique

THERE are more schools of thought in piano study than there are religions; like religions, each school claims to be the one and only.

In this book, because we are amateurs whose goal is to enrich ourselves musically, I have placed repertoire first and technique second. It's a sound sequence for us to follow, especially as my treatment of fractures makes of each fracture a technical problem which must not only be solved but conquered. Each fracture you set smooths the way for easier setting of other fractures which contain similar difficulties. That this mode of procedure brings about consistent technical advancement is a truth you will realize before you have been at this work two months. If, not having tried it out yet, you are unconvinced, I don't ask you to take my word. I will merely mention the names of four pianists who believe in, and apply, the theory of getting all their technical work from the pieces they play; I know this because they have told me so. Their names are Sascha Gorodnitzki, Shura Cherkassky, Alexander Brailowsky, and Vladimir Horowitz.

It is not a method, however, that I advance as the one and only. The more technique you acquire the better you will be able to play and the more you will enjoy playing. I have suggested that you use only ten minutes a day for technical work; but if it suited your time and your pianistic ambition to work a daily hour at technique along with a daily hour at repertoire, I would applaud like a one-man claque.

Improvement in technical ability is a curiously interesting process to observe when it is happening to oneself. Things that used to be formidable become easy. Ferruccio Busoni, when thought to be at the height of his powers, devoted two years almost exclusively to technical study. At the conclusion of this period he stated: "To my great delight, details that had always defied me, the rebellious trills, the faltering bravura passages, the uneven runs, all came into beautiful submission and with them came a new delight in playing." Mark Hambourg writes inspiringly in his book *How to Play the Piano:* "There is no greater suffering than to have in the mind a certain impression which music has created in it, and not be able to reproduce this impression on the piano because of shortcomings in technique. On the other hand, what joy it is to a pianist to resume the playing of some masterpiece, which he had studied diligently in former years and to which at that time had never succeeded in giving the rendering that he sought, owing to insufficient mastery of means. But upon starting it again after this long period during which he has been developing gradually, he finds that now he can at last do with ease what he wants in the piece which he never could arrive at before. To attain such a reward is worth all the labors of Hercules!"

On my modest scale, I have had identical experiences. And it was David Warfield, the great actor, who, in the course of an interview, stated the truth of the matter with absolute exactness. I was questioning him about his extraordinarily successful interpretation of his greatest role, Herr Anton von Barwig in *The Music Master.* "Was it hard?" I asked. I still see vividly the white-haired, linen-suited old gentleman smoking his long cigar in the August heat as we sat in his Central Park West apartment; he listened to my question, smiled gently, and said: "Nothing that you can do is hard." I have long pondered that answer. It applies equally to a beginner realizing that he can at last successfully add his left hand to his right in playing a scale; to a more advanced student playing a Mendelssohn *Song Without Words* well; to a still more advanced student playing a

Bach fugue well; to a run-of-the-mill concert pianist playing Schumann's *Carnaval* well; to Josef Hofmann playing the *Don Juan Fantasy* of Liszt. . . .

But it is my duty to warn you that preoccupation with technique can be carried too far. It is my duty to tell you how, ·by working too earnestly at technique, I shattered the nerves of three distinguished metropolitan journalists.

The editorial offices of *The New Yorker* are on the nineteenth floor of a drafty, macabre building on West Forty-third Street. Some years ago the editors had the bright idea of taking a small suite of rooms on the seventeenth floor and placing therein certain gregariously-inclined writers who, when on the nineteenth floor, had a tendency to sit around by the hour and discuss current events. The theory of the editors was that these writers, if banished to a sparsely populated suite below stairs, would develop a tendency to get some writing done. (To this day, the editors don't know that the net result was that the banished writers sat around for even longer hours and, without any danger of being overheard, discussed the editors, disparagingly.)

I was one of the banished writers. But the group never gathered in my room, because it had the reputation of being haunted. At that time I had a small silent keyboard, on which, when not engaged in interviewing or in the hateful labor of setting down the results of interviews, I used to snatch odd moments of technical practice. These keyboards are called silent, but the truth is they make an unsettling noise—a subtle clicking not unlike tappings at a séance. The desk in the room next to mine is just opposite the spot where I placed my keyboard. The three ace journalists I'm talking about— St. Clair McKelway, Jack Alexander, and A. J. Liebling—sat at this desk in succession and honestly tried to work. I would hear the typewriter going great guns as I sat down to knock off a little sly hobby work. I would start. The typewriter would immediately stop. Then it would start again, falteringly. Then I would start again and again it would stop—in the middle of a quotation mark. After a few days of this, each of these journalists—the best of good fellows, though high-strung—gave up. They never opened my door to see what was making the horrid little noise. My theory is they were afraid to; I think they thought it was the ticking of a time bomb. Anyway, I met McKelway in the hall as he was moving out. "Where you going?" I said. "I—I've decided to go back upstairs," he said. His face was haggard. Jack Alexander tried the desk next. Four days later he, too, was gone. I met him at a cocktail party soon after. "What happened to you?" I said, jovially. "I'm working at home now," he said, edging away from me.

Once, after finishing an especially satisfactory practice session, I heard a furtive step. Opening my door, I saw Jim Thurber, who had been in the next room. He gave a little scream when he saw me and hurried toward the elevator. Late that evening, I am told, he was heard singing the *Internationale* all by himself in the Algonquin lobby. That was the first and the last time that the Nestor of *New Yorker* writers ever ventured down to the seventeenth floor.

A. J. Liebling, the next occupant, was the only one of my victims who tried to fight back. For the first two days my practicing had only the typical effect of astonishing his typewriter into silence. But on the third day, after I had practiced a certain *rat-ta-tat-tat*, I heard an answering *rat-ta-tat-tat* from his room. I went *rat-ta-tat*. Back came *rat-ta-tat*. I played a solitary *tat*. *Tat* came from Liebling's room. This insane fugue went on for five minutes. Then I shut my keyboard with a bang, went out of my room, and opened Liebling's door. He rose slowly from a kneeling position. "What the hell are you doing?" I said, looking like Boris Karloff. I knew perfectly well what he was doing: he was tapping on the baseboard with a pencil. "What the hell are *you* doing?" he said, weakly. The very next morning, he boarded a Lisbon-bound Clipper to become *The New Yorker*'s Paris correspondent. While over there he took part in the evacuation of Paris and was bombed twice, but his dispatches were notable for their balance, judiciousness, wisdom, and the inimitable Liebling humor. When he got back, I said, "How was France, Joe?" "Fine," he said, "and I'm taking the room on the *other* side of you." He did. David Lardner, Ring Lardner's son, now sits at that desk. But it is no longer hexed, because I don't practice on my keyboard any more. I feel, if only because of my loyalty to *The New Yorker*, that it is wrong to unstring that magazine's crack writers.

And I also feel, now, that practicing on a silent keyboard is carrying a hobby too far.

Where were we?

Oh yes—for our purposes, whatever the time we choose to give to technical work, let us think of it as consisting of (*a*) scales and arpeggios, and (*b*) special exercises.

### *a.*
### Scales and arpeggios

Josef Lhevinne: "The highest technique, broadly speaking, may be traced back to scales and arpeggios. And the practice of scales and arpeggios need never be mechanical or uninteresting."

Wilhelm Bachaus: "I reiterate with all possible emphasis that the source of my technical equipment is scales, scales, scales. I find their continued daily practice not only beneficial, but necessary."

Nicholas Rubinstein: "Scales should never be dry. If you are not interested in them, work with them until you become interested in them."

Ernest Hutcheson: "The experienced teacher knows that a fluency and an ease and a general intuitive intimacy with the keyboard can be obtained through the use of scales and arpeggios that cannot be obtained as easily in any other way."

Vladimir de Pachmann: "Take the scale of C major, for instance. This scale is by far the most difficult of all. The scale of C should be learned step by step until the practice habits are so formed that they will reign supreme while playing all the other scales."

It is beneficial to play scales—major, melodic minor, and harmonic minor—in all keys, for four octaves, with both hands, in the intervals of the octave, third, tenth (which is only an expanded third), and sixth. Also in contrary motion for three octaves.

Scales may be varied interestingly by playing them slowly, rapidly, legato, staccato, in various dynamic intensities, with *crescendo* and *diminuendo* shadings, emphasizing right hand, emphasizing left hand. They should be played in various rhythms. I have found the following rhythms useful when playing scales for four octaves:

1.

2.

3.

4.

5.

The obvious way to use these rhythms is to select one of them and play a scale—say C or E—to this rhythm, in both hands, successively in the octave, third, tenth, and sixth intervals. A less obvious and more useful way is to select two of these rhythms, say 1 and 2, and play your scale using Rhythm 1 in the right hand and Rhythm 2 in the left. Then change hands, taking Rhythm 2 in the right and Rhythm 1 in the left. Then try Rhythm 1 and Rhythm 3. Rhythms 4 and 5 can be similarly combined. Playing rhythms against each other in this way adds practice in independent finger action to practice in new rhythmic designs. A word of caution:

playing rhythms against each other is best begun when your mind is clear as a bell. Soon it becomes easier, however, and provides a refreshingly new aspect to scale practice.

Scales in contrary motion, three octaves, may be played in the following rhythmic groupings of three notes—and so can scales in parallel motion, played for three octaves instead of four:

1.

2.

3.

4.

5.

(Try combining Rhythms 2 and 3.)

Arpeggios—major, minor, dominant seventh, and diminished seventh—may be practiced in as many different ways as scales.

Passing the thumb under correctly is of the utmost importance in both scales and arpeggios, but in the latter it requires greater care and precision because the intervals are wider. Katherine Ruth Heyman calls arpeggios "scales in seven-league boots."

The finest book in existence on the subject of scales and arpeggios is *Mastering the Scales and Arpeggios*,* by James Francis Cooke, editor of *The Etude* and, I'm sorry to say, no relation to me. Get a copy of this book and you'll find that if I haven't convinced you that scale-and-arpeggio practice can be extremely interesting, Dr. Cooke will. His vigorous, definitive volume begins with a history of scales, followed by an exposition of their structure. The bulk of *Mastering the Scales and Arpeggios* consists of the scales and arpeggios themselves, written out in all their many varieties and carefully fingered; together with exercises in passing the thumb under, which, if sedulously practiced, will quickly improve your facility in this all-important skill. In particular, I recommend that you practice the thumb exercise devised by Kalkbrenner which Dr. Cooke prints on page 11. Pages 33 and 34 present interesting ways of combining third, tenth, and sixth scale playing with contrary as well as parallel motion.

If you are at all shaky on the fingering of scales as you take them up seriously again, Dr. Cooke gives, on page 10, a single explanatory column which reduces

* Published by the Theodore Presser Company, 1712 Chestnut Street, Philadelphia, Pa.; $1.50.

scale fingering to the simplest and most easily remembered system I have ever seen. I suggest that, as a preliminary, you study and absorb this system.

Dr. Cooke gives you a choice of three fingerings for the chromatic scale—French, English, and German (or Mixed)—but by placing the French fingering first in all his examples he implies that he prefers it to the others. This is the system in which the third finger of both hands is on all black keys, the thumb of the right hand on all white keys except C and F (which are played with the second finger) and the thumb of the left hand on all white keys except B and E (second finger). I have found that most teachers and most pianists favor this fingering for the chromatic scale.

Pages 36 and 37 provide material for playing scales with various accents—all of them different from those I recommend a few pages back.

You have, of course, at one time or another watched a friend play scales faster than you can—and you envied him his skill. And that friend has, of course, at one time or another watched a friend of *his* play scales still faster—and envied him his skill. I have, of course, many times watched friends of mine play scales faster than I can—and envied them their skill. All of which is by way of stating a universal truth of music study: seeing someone play scales faster than we can always arouses the desire to be able to go and do likewise. Dr. Cooke provides, on pages 51 and 52 of his book, the best method I have yet encountered for increasing one's velocity in scale playing. It involves the use of "Pier Notes" (an invention of Dr. Cooke) and should not be taken up until you have practiced straight scale playing for many months. You will find that after a few weeks with Dr. Cooke's Pier Notes your scales will make your friends envy you.

The material on arpeggios in *Mastering the Scales and Arpeggios* includes some excellent special exercises. One is the series of five exercises for "Expanding the Hand without Injury"—useful for any hand, but especially useful for small hands which are graduating from scale work to the wider reaches of arpeggio work. Others are the "Arpeggio Variants" exercises, beginning on pages 65, 67, 73, and, concluding the book, on page 79.

Arpeggios, like scales, should be practiced in various rhythms as well as "straight." I recommend applying to arpeggios the rhythms suggested for scales (turn back to pages 133 and 134), and combining them in the two hands in the same way.

## Scales in double thirds

The practice of scales in double thirds provides far greater benefits to the fingers and to one's technique in general than plain scales. Our weak fingers are the fourth and fifth. In plain scales, the fourth is used (usually) only once in each octave, the fifth only at the bottom of the left-hand scale and the top of the right-hand scale. In some plain scales, the fifth finger is not used at all. In double-third scales, however, the fourth and fifth fingers are used constantly and, which is of equal importance, each tone of the scale is a two-note chord, requiring both co-operation between the fingers and independence of the fingers.

Dr. Cooke writes out all major and harmonic minor scales in double thirds, but in this one instance I do not follow his fingerings. For double-third major and harmonic minor scales, I use Tobias Matthay's system of fingering, which was taught me by James Friskin, who studied with Matthay. Once you have mastered the not-difficult knack of sliding the thumb over adjacent white keys, the Matthay system makes for unusual legato and speed. I suggest that you buy the "Practice Card" for "Double-Third Scales—Their Fingering and Practice" by Matthay.* This, a single piece of cardboard printed on both sides, contains the Matthay fingering system for double-third scales in major and harmonic minor forms, together with instructions for practicing them.

* Send to the Arthur P. Schmidt Company, 120 Boylston Street, Boston, Mass.; 65¢

Matthay's practice card also includes chromatic double-third scales, but in this one instance I part company with him on fingering, as I do with Dr. Cooke on the fingering of major and harmonic minor double-third scales.

After years of study of the fingerings recommended by Chopin, Moszkowski, Matthay, Cortot, and Godowsky, for chromatic scales in minor and major double thirds, I have evolved—borrowing here and slightly

### Chromatic Double Minor Thirds

### Chromatic Double Major Thirds

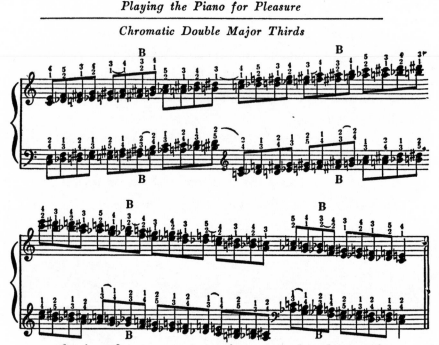

altering there—a system of my own for these scales. It is based largely on the systems of these masters; it has proved to be highly practicable, and it is a *single* system. All the works on the subject which I have studied give a variety (usually bewildering) of alternative fingerings. I have written out my composite system for two octaves here, but it is to be practiced, of course, for four octaves in parallel motion and for three in contrary motion. Minor chromatic thirds are given first because they are encountered much more often in piano literature than major chromatic thirds.

These two fingerings, for minor and major, are closely related. They are, in fact, reducible to a startlingly simple formula, which you can use to impress them more deeply on your mind (if you decide to adopt them), and to check yourself as you practice. "Outer" notes are the right hand's upper notes, the left hand's lower; "inner" notes are vice versa. This is the formula:

All outer black notes, 3; all inner black notes, 2; outer white notes, 4, except 5 on F and C in the right hand and on E and B in the left hand; inner white notes, thumb, with these exceptions—

minor, right hand ascending
minor and major, left hand ascending $\Big\}$ 2 on E and B

minor, right hand descending
minor and major, left hand descending $\Big\}$ 2 on C and F

When playing any scale in double thirds, remember and apply Godowsky's advice to "keep the fingers 'glued to the keys.' " Hand and fingers should be very relaxed: relax them consciously before you start and test your relaxation periodically as you practice. If hand or fingers are stiff, you will find these fingerings impossible; they can only be used when accompanied by relaxation. Incline the hand slightly in the direction in which you are playing. If you've never tried double-third scales, don't handicap yourself by thinking they are very difficult. You will find them less difficult than you had imagined. Take a few notes and practice them very slowly in the right hand, gradually increasing speed. Then take the parallel left-hand passage and practice it the same way. Put the two together. Do this until you have a complete octave in both hands. From this it is easy to extend a scale in double thirds to four octaves. Finally, practice these scales in various rhythms and combinations of rhythms.

When playing the chromatic scale in minor double thirds, note that there are two places in each octave where two black notes are played together. Katherine Ruth Heyman calls these, appropriately, "bridges"; they are marked "B" in the examples shown; and the fingering is always $\frac{3}{2}$ in the right hand and $\frac{2}{3}$ in the left. They are useful landmarks. Note, too, that in the ascending right hand and the descending left hand, the third *after* the bridge is always fingered with the fourth and second fingers: the second finger *slides* from a black note to a white. Note that two fingerings at the top of the right hand have been circled in the minor scale: this is to emphasize the slight fingering change that is necessary when the right hand rounds the pylon and starts back down.

When playing the chromatic scale in double major thirds, note that there is only one "bridge" per octave and that the sliding of the second finger is reversed: in this scale the second finger is slid when the right hand descends and when the left hand ascends. In the chromatic scale of major thirds, the thumb has the task of sliding (in the ascending right hand and descending left hand) from one white note to another. Holding the wrist a little higher than usual at these points will facilitate this. You might also take note of the fact that —in the ascending right hand and descending left hand —*every inner white note of the chromatic scale in double major thirds is taken by the thumb.*

Practicing chromatic double thirds in contrary motion is useful. For minor thirds, I suggest starting with the right hand $\frac{4}{2}$ on G sharp–B at the center of the keyboard, the left hand $\frac{2}{4}$ on F–A flat; in other words, the second fingers of your two hands will be on the same note: G sharp–A flat. This may seem cramping, but five seconds, on an average, are required to get used to it. Having got used to it, play the scale for three octaves, returning to the same note. For major thirds, this can be done similarly by taking A flat–C with the right hand's $\frac{5}{2}$ and E–G sharp with the left hand's $\frac{2}{5}$. By using these starting points, fingering in the two hands will always be the same at any given point in either the minor or major scale in chromatic double thirds. After a few months, begin using the three-note rhythms given on page 134.

## *b.*
## Special exercises

When Ferruccio Busoni wrote, "Don't think of the keyboard as a kind of gymnasium attached to a musical instrument," he was not inveighing against technical exercises. In fact he wrote elsewhere how, in the two years of diligent work during which he revolutionized his technique, he used special exercises of his own devising. No, Busoni meant what Josef Hofmann meant when the latter wrote calling for "A larger participation of the mind in the acquisition of technique."

Concentrate as you work on them, and technical exercises can be completely absorbing; the more your mind participates in this work, the less the keyboard is a mere digital gymnasium.

An absolutely splendid book for any pianist who wants to tone up and improve his technique is C. L. Hanon's famous *The Virtuoso Pianist*. Students and artists refer to this work by the Napoleonically simple title of "Hanon." As its own preface states, "This work is intended for all piano pupils. It may be taken up after the pupil has studied about a year." Sergei Rachmaninoff once said: "In the Imperial music schools of Russia, the student got most of his technical instruction for the first five years from Hanon; in fact, this was practically the only book of strictly technical exercises employed."

Hanon comes in three separate volumes, also in one book * which includes all three. Rachmaninoff referred of course to the inclusive book, which is the one you should get. I suggest working as the instructions indicate and then, after a few months, begin transposing them and also playing them in the various rhythms listed on page 133. Used in rhythms and in transposition, they are at their maximum value. The fact that the book's instructions don't mention transposing them is just one of those stupendous mysteries like the Riddle of the Universe or the Loch Ness monster. A good way to begin transposing Hanon is to do the first exercise in Book I in G, then the second in F. Note how adding only one black key radically changes, and renders more complex and therefore more beneficial, these exercises.

After working with Hanon for a year or two, transposing and rhythmically complicating them, you will

* C. L. Hanon, *The Virtuoso Pianist* (Schirmer); $1.75.

want to get a book that is indispensable if you wish to extract the last drops of juice out of Hanon's extraordinarily juicy opus. I am referring to Orville A. Lindquist's *Technical Variants on Hanon's Exercises.*† The preface of this book states: "The first book of C. L. Hanon's *The Virtuoso Pianist* is unquestionably the most universally used book of finger technics that we have. Excellent as these studies are, it is the feeling of the author that in order to get the best results from them they should be practiced in all keys and with various rhythms; hence this work." Whereupon Professor Lindquist proceeds to devise rhythms of every conceivable kind for all the exercises in Hanon's first book. The result is a marvel of ingenuity and several years of productive practice for you and me. Since you will presumably own a complete Hanon before you get Professor Lindquist's volume, and since he concerns himself only with Book I, I suggest that you may want to carry on by complicating the following additional Hanon exercises according to the Lindquist rhythmic twists: exercises 21 through 31 and exercises 42 and 43 in Book II; exercises 49 and 59 in Book III.

Such adventures are getting pretty far along the road of advanced technique. Let's turn to some exercises

† The Arthur P. Schmidt Co., 120 Boylston Street, Boston, Mass.; 75¢.

which lay a firm foundation for advanced technique. Here are some of the technical exercises which James Friskin, without claiming authorship of them, recommends to his pupils. No other exercises that I have encountered will do as much, in as short a time, toward starching and stiffening your technique. In all cases, fingerings above the notes are for the right hand, those below the notes for the left:

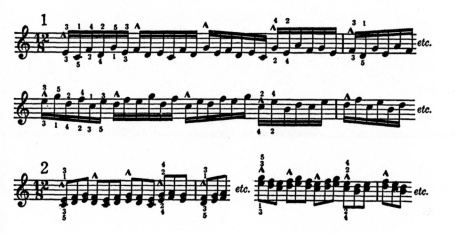

Play 1 and 2 up and down one octave, as shown. Take them separately at first; slowly; playing firmly with relaxed, "dead-weight" fingers, and relaxed wrist and arm; accent the first note of each group of six notes in 1 and three notes in 2. Rotate the relaxed wrist laterally as you play; this may be done more easily in 1 than in

2, but be sure that, having practiced it thoroughly in 1, you apply this rotation to 2. Next (still sticking to the key of C) practice the exercises in the following rhythms:

For exercise 1:

For exercise 2:

In the preceding rhythms, the second is more difficult than the first in both cases: the trick is to place the accent successfully on the short opening note of each group.

Mr. Friskin recommends transposing these exercises to E flat and to E. You may wish to transpose them to

the other major keys. If you do that, try them also in
C minor: the digital difficulties will immediately become
greater, likewise the resultant digital benefits.

These exercises may also be played, say two years
from now (if you are now undertaking them for the
first time), on the chords of the diminished seventh and
the dominant seventh, moving chromatically up and
down. In this form (below), they are a superior
"stretching exercise" for the fingers. But beware lest
you strain your fingers: stop at the first feeling of
strain.

The following is an excellent exercise in broken-arpeggio playing. Practice it at first very slowly, hands separately, using Miss Heyman's Triple Stroke which is described on page 63. Rotate the relaxed wrist laterally even more than you did in exercises 1 and 2. Then put the hands together, continuing to use the Triple Stroke. Finally play it, hands together, as written. Transpose it to all major and minor keys. Throughout, let the top note of the ascending passage and the bottom note of the descending passage "throw" your relaxed arm off the keyboard with a stroke of (ascending) the right-hand fifth finger and left-hand thumb and (descending) the right-hand thumb and left-hand fifth. In different keys, the use of your third and fourth fingers will not always be the same as that shown in the C-major example, which follows:

Now we come to another very useful, but totally different, exercise recommended by Mr. Friskin. Hold the eighth notes firmly, but don't tighten the hand.

Play the sixteenth notes firmly, but don't tighten the hand. It is a good idea to practice this exercise a long time with the hands separately before putting the hands together. Transpose to E flat and E and any other keys you wish to, preferably all other major keys:

After a while, extend the finger action of this exercise. by practicing it in the following rhythm:

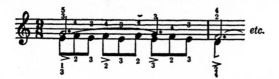

The following is an octave exercise, though written in single notes. Play it only in the key of C for a long time, first the right hand, then the left hand, then the hands together. Count the time slowly enough in the first measure to ensure being able to play the entire exercise in correct time. Relax your arm and hand for all you're worth on the first and third beats of each measure. If you transpose, use the fifth finger always on the black notes: this is a staccato octave exercise. Plenty of ways to practice legato octaves, using the fourth finger on black notes, will be found in Dr. Cooke's *Mastering the Scales and Arpeggios.* Here, then, is the octave exercise which Mr. Friskin's pupils practice:

As you increase speed, *think* the fast octaves in a rush (being careful to keep accurate time), and they'll soon be playing in a rush, and your octave technique will be faster than it ever was before. (The double dots at the beginning and end of measures, in this and later exercises, mean that the measures are to be repeated.)

You may remember my mentioning that Alexander Brailowsky believes in letting repertoire practice supply technical practice. Nevertheless, just before his recitals, he does a technical exercise of his own as a warmer-up. Here, with the artist's permission, it is:

*and so on,
chromatically
up and down—*

(I recommend practicing Brailowsky's exercise alternately staccato and legato.)

Walter Gieseking once made the following statement: "The most difficult thing about learning to play the piano is training the fingers to play evenly, because they are of different strengths. But once that has become automatic, the rest is a matter for the brain." None of us is going to develop fingers that play as evenly as Walter Gieseking's. But we can act on his advice, and there is a very good book—or rather two books, Part I and Part II—which plays right into our hands, or at least into our fingers. This is Isidor Philipp's great *Exercises for Independence of the Fingers.*\* Part I of this work is likely to be more useful to the amateur, Part II being rather terrifyingly advanced. The exercises are set down in groups called Series. In Part I, I recommend the following Series, complete: 1st, 2nd, 4th, and 6th. I recommend exercises 7 through 15 in the 12th Series and 11 through 15 in the 14th Series. Series 4, which consists of 35 separate exercises, is, for my money, the best single technical drill for the piano that has ever been penned. I recommend taking Series 4 very slowly—which Mr. Philipp also recommends by his tempo indication of "*Lento.*" And I recommend holding the held fingers firmly, then sounding the next two beats once staccato, followed by once legato.

Brahms wrote a book of technical exercises † which, being excellent, deserve to be better known and more widely used. I am continually asking piano students "Have you ever used Brahms' exercises?" and continually getting "No; I didn't know he wrote any" for an answer. Several concert pianists, even, have professed ignorance of these exercises. Odd that technical studies by the composer who, in his Paganini Variations, carried piano technique to its highest peak, should be.

\* G. Schirmer; each part $1.10.

† *Brahms 51 Ubungen,* Edition Breitkopf; send to G. Schirmer, New York; $1.25.

so little known! I recommend these exercises for all who
wish to go on with advanced technical study. They are
difficult, but not forbiddingly difficult; and they are all
economical of your time and extraordinarily beneficial
to your skill. Two of these exercises, No. 8 and No. 30,
tower above the others in usefulness and I am therefore
reprinting them, complete. They are aimed, with deadly
accuracy, at the weaknesses of our fourth and fifth
fingers.

Take especial care about the accurate and smooth
passing of the thumb under the fourth finger, after
No. 8, going from $\frac{2}{4}$ into $\frac{3}{4}$ time, becomes more extended.

Ultimately—but don't attempt it until you have
practiced No. 30 in its original form for many months
—practice it in the $\frac{9}{8}$ rhythm shown on page 151. When

you can play No. 30 through once, using this $\frac{9}{8}$ rhythm,
without unduly tiring your fourth and fifth fingers,

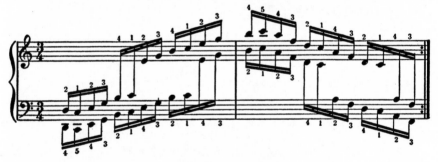

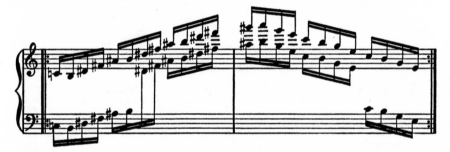

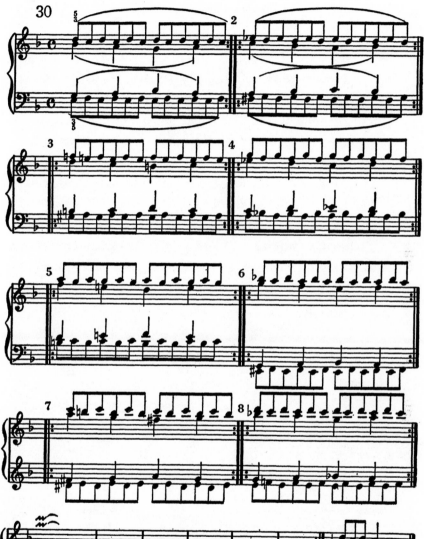

you'll have far stronger-than-average fourth and fifth fingers.

Chopin's Etude in A minor, Op. 10, No. 2, is when played in recital undoubtedly the supreme test of strong and agile fourth and fifth fingers of the right hand. It is superb for strengthening these fingers when practiced by pianists whose technical skill is still at an intermediate stage. We must remember that although Chopin's Etudes are music of the finest type, he wrote them for the purpose that their name describes: as technical studies. One way to use the Op. 10, No. 2 Etude is to take only the first four measures, strip off the left hand (which is only accompaniment), and practice these measures over and over for weeks. Play the third, fourth, and fifth fingers firmly and as legato as possible.

Play the accompanying $\dfrac{2}{1}$ chord clearly but staccato.

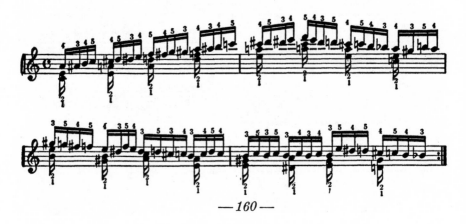

Keep the hand as relaxed as in double-third scales. Turn the wrist slightly to the right, both ascending and descending; this assists the fingers. Use all the rhythms listed on page 133.

After a few weeks, add more measures. Then more. Then play the right hand of the entire piece, still slowly. Finally add the left hand. Don't feel you're losing pianistic face by continuing to play slowly: taken at full speed, this is a virtuoso piece of terrifying difficulty.

What about the left hand? James Friskin wrote out for me a similar left-hand exercise and I have expanded it into one for both hands, which may be quickly memorized. It develops the fourth and fifth fingers of both hands, as Chopin's Etude develops them in the right hand. Here it is written out for one octave in the key of C:

I practiced this exercise for two months in C, hands separately, very slowly, and for one octave. Then I put the hands together, expanded to two octaves, to three. Then I transposed it to D flat, a process which in itself took me a daily quarter of an hour for a week. Now I practice it in all major keys, moving chromatically upward from C to C; and in various rhythms. In each new key the fingers move differently in relation to the accompanying chords. I find D flat and F sharp the most difficult keys and suggest that you might skip them, as I often do. Always, ascending and descending, turn the right hand slightly to the right, the left hand slightly to the left. Transposing will be facilitated if you remember these things: the running passage is a simple chromatic scale; on beat two of the first measure and beat two of the second measure the two hands play identical chords; the fingering is standard in all keys— third finger always on all black notes in both hands— fourth finger on all white notes in the right hand except C and F which take the fifth—fourth finger on all white notes in the left hand except B and E which take the fifth—accompanying staccato chords always played by the first and second fingers in both hands, except the first and the last which (because the thumbs would collide) are a single note, taken by the second finger in each hand.

"But you haven't even mentioned Czerny!" you exclaim. True. We are searching for ways to warm, not chill, our music-making. The best explanation I ever heard of why Czerny wrote his millions of dry notes was that which Anton Rubinstein told Egon Petri that Moritz Moszkowski gave: "Czerny hated little children."

# 5

## Sight Reading

In the books on piano playing I have read, I have found much dogmatic and ill-humored divergence of opinion. All the authors had the commendable aim of bettering piano playing; most of them had important and interesting things to say; but their capacity for agreement equaled, approximately, that of Democrats and Republicans.

Except on one point: sight reading.

Without a single exception, the authors took this stand:

"The best way to develop your sight reading is to sight-read."

With this stand I align myself, heart and soul.

Having thus jumped on the bandwagon, I will confine myself to suggestions as to how to go about developing your sight reading by sight reading.

I suggest that you go through all the music on your

piano and make a pile of that which you don't expect to study for your repertoire.

I suggest that you look inside your piano bench for further ammunition for the campaign.

I suggest you search your attic.

I suggest, if you find yourself short of sight-reading material of your own, that you snoop around the visible music in your friends' homes and ask if you may borrow a batch of unused single pieces or albums.

(I suggest you return this borrowed music within a reasonable time.)

I suggest, in a word, that you make as big a pile of music for sight reading as you can. Do you remember how, as a child, you sometimes raked together an absolutely stupendous pile of autumn leaves? Let the same delicious urge motivate you again. This time it will be to more purpose.

My own sight-reading pile stands hip-high and I expect to have read my way through it by 1998, at which time I will be ninety-four years old. This pile, among thousands of other items, contains Haydn sonatas; various popular songs including *In My Tip Tip Tippy Canoe* and *Just Like Washington Crossed the Delaware, Gen. Pershing Will Cross the Rhine;* older songs, such as *Are You Not a Coquette, Lulu Darling?* and *Father Is Drinking Again;* a hymnal; the

*Buttermilk and Praties Jig,* the *Jock o' Hazledean Fling, Miss McLeod's Reel,* the *Paddy O' Snap Strathspey,* the *Looney MacTwolter Hornpipe,* and assorted polkas, quadrilles, schottisches, and galops; a composition by Weber (H. Weber) entitled *The Storm—An Imitation of Nature* and containing this direction: "The loud pedal is to be held down throughout the piece"; and *Liebestraum* by one Franz Liszt, embellished by a vocal lyric ("My dream of love") by Jerry Castillo and ukelele chords by Jim Smock.

I nibble at my pile at the rate of ten minutes a day— ten minutes a day—never less and never more. If this persists in seeming a short period to you, please to remember what I mentioned earlier: ten minutes a day is sixty hours a year, 300 hours in five years, and 600 hours in ten. I've been sight reading thus for three years (180 hours) and can report that my sight reading has improved markedly: partly through practice and partly through sheer amazement at what my moving eye encounters.

If you have never done any systematic sight reading, the best way to begin is to place a piece of new music in front of you and sit quietly with your hands in your lap. I'm not being flip. I mean just what I say. Keep your hands in your lap and take a good long look at the music. Look at it as hard as the elder Mr. Weller looked at Sam Weller and Mr. Pickwick: "At last the stout man began to puff at his pipe without leaving off at all and to stare at the newcomers as if he had made up his mind to see the most he could of them." Note carefully the piece's name, tempo indication, key and time signature; then mentally read through the first few measures to get the rhythm and, as much as you are able to divine without playing, the melody.

Then go to it, always being more concerned to keep the rhythm going than to play the right notes. In fact, in sight reading let wrong notes fall under the piano until the floor is ankle deep with them—if that is necessary to keep a piece's time beats surging along without a break.

It is a good idea, too, to keep the left hand going at the expense of the right, if necessary—but almost never vice versa. The foundation of music is the bass.

Cultivate the habit of reading not individual notes but, insofar as you can, groups of notes.

Read ahead as far as you safely can.

Don't bother about fingering at all.

Don't look down at the keyboard any more than you can help. Some teachers say: "*Never* look down at the keyboard while sight reading." This is hogwash: the teachers themselves look down occasionally while sight reading: it is impossible not to. But look down only when absolutely necessary. Get out of the bad sight-reading habit which I call the "marionette nod."

Get to know leger lines as familiarly as you know the staff's FACE spaces and EGBDF lines.

The more you work on your repertoire, the more your technical ability will improve—which will in turn improve your sight-reading ability, through increased facility in translating printed notes into played notes. The more you sight-read, the easier the preliminary stages of repertoire practice will become—through increased familiarity with keys, accidentals, rhythms, chords, and passage-work patterns. A benign circle.

Accompany singers and instrumentalists every chance you get—and when doing so, keep an ear cocked on the soloist, so that your playing follows him while it supports him. This is one of the pleasantest ways to sight-read, though you'll have to be even more alert than when you're sight reading alone in the privacy of your music room.

One of the deepest satisfactions that follows improvement in one's playing is improvement in one's sight reading. And nowhere is this satisfaction deeper than in sessions of ensemble music in the home. Nothing develops sight reading so delightfully as getting a group of amateurs together with some unfamiliar music and letting the devil take the hindmost.

## 6

# A Discussion of Certain
# Fine Compositions
*(Arranged approximately in order of difficulty)*

1. Chopin—Prelude in A, Op. 28, No. 7
2. Bach—Prelude in C from *The Well-Tempered Clavichord*
3. Beethoven—Minuet in G
4. Grieg—Nocturne, Op. 54, No. 4
5. Chopin—Mazurka in A minor, Op. 68, No. 2 (posthumous)
6. Liszt—*Consolation* No. 3
7. Debussy—*Danseuses de Delphes*
8. Mendelssohn—Scherzo in E minor, Op. 16, No. 2
9. Debussy—*Clair de lune*
10. Chopin—Nocturne in F sharp, Op. 15, No. 2

## 1. Chopin—Prelude in A, Op. 28, No. 7

James Huneker found this prelude "mazurka-like, a silhouette of the natural dance." Other commentators think of it as an outline of the waltz. Mazurka or waltz, it is certainly in three-four time. Be sure, therefore, that you feel its three-four rhythm accurately. Resist the temptation to accent the *Auftakt*. Pupils averse to "counting" sometimes produce even this:

etc.

I incline to the waltz conception and always put the accent—such as it is—on the first beat of every measure. I say "such as it is" because it should never be a sharp accent: it should be more felt than sounded, more "leaned on" than struck.

The climax is, of course, the half-note chord that opens measure 12. In many editions—including the Schirmer collected Preludes edited by Joseffy—this all-important, climactic, strong chord is marked to be played thus: left hand, F sharp, C sharp, E, F sharp; right hand, A sharp, C sharp, E, A sharp, C sharp—exasperatingly difficult for any hands smaller than Primo Carnera's.

To mention only two bad musical by-products of this distribution of notes: the right hand's thumb has to sound both an A sharp and a C sharp simultaneously (one or the other of these notes is sure to be slighted). Also the top A sharp and C sharp, which need most strength because they are in the piano's higher, weaker range, are taken respectively by the weak fourth finger and the weak fifth, which are further weakened by the pianistically unnatural stretching of the entire hand.

I suggest, for this chord, the masterly redistribution of notes which is shown in the Joseffy-Schirmer edition of the separate prelude (printed together with the Prelude in B minor, No. 6):

I don't know why there are two versions by the same editor and the same publishing house, but I know which fingering version I prefer for this chord.

The composition is divided into equal halves. Make it sound this way by an almost imperceptible pause at the line of demarkation, just after beat 2 in measure 8. Savor the added alto G sharp in the opening of the second half: it adds tang, as compared with the solo C sharp in measure 1.

The alto voice of beat 3 in measure 13 and beats 1 and 2 in measures 14—A and G sharp—provide a good opportunity to bring out a plaintive, significant inner voice.

### Probable fractures:

None, except the climactic chord which can be set in half a minute by using Joseffy's redistribution of notes just discussed.

### Memory aids:

The similarities—and differences—between the corresponding measures of the first half and the second half of the composition.

The line of the deepest bass notes—E A E A E A B A. Think of them in pairs: E A; E A; E A; B A.

In measure four's opening chord, the second finger of the right hand, holding C sharp, and the thumb of the left hand, holding E, are holding the notes of the second chord in this measure. Note this with your eye. Note, too, that the first chord is actually the second chord with an A added above and an A added below.

## 2. Bach—Prelude in C from
### *The Well-Tempered Clavichord*

It is divided into three parts—measures 1–11, 12–19, and 20–35. The third part is actually a long coda.

At first glance so simple, this composition is in reality not simple at all. No two consecutive measures have the same harmonic content and there is much dynamic variety before the climactic measure 29 (usually played *ff* for the first two beats, followed by a *diminuendo* to measure 33 beginning with beats 3 and 4).

When beginning to practice this piece, count the opening two or three measures with rigid accuracy for a while, accenting each 1, 2, 3, 4 (left hand, right hand, left hand, right hand) until you get the rhythmic pulse beating correctly. Finally only "feel" the pulse as you play. Strangely, considering the simplicity of the figure on which this piece is based

it is easy to distort rhythmically.

Busoni says: no pedal until bar 24, pedal twice per measure from 24 to 28, once per measure from 28 to the end. As part of Busoni's gradual "thickening" of the timbre of this piece, he recommends holding, in measures 20 through 23, not only the left-hand notes but the right-hand notes as well.

As to the tempo, editors disagree. Czerny indicates

*allegro*, Busoni *moderato*, and Frederick Iliff (M.A., Mus. Doc., Oxon.) *andante con moto*. I think it preferable to walk the conservative middle of the road, with Busoni.

If your edition of this prelude contains 36 measures, cross out measure 23 with a very black pencil. Musicologists are in practically unanimous agreement that this famous disputed measure is spurious, having been inserted by an indelicate gentleman named Schwenke. Nobody wants to play, in the heart of 35 measures of *urtext* Bach, even one measure by Schwenke.

### Probable fractures:

None, unless, in measures 33 and 34, the sudden change from the typical figure makes it advisable to go over these measures a few times to drill them into your fingers.

### Memory aids:

Mark off the three parts with double bar lines.

Memorize the chordal structure before memorizing in final form.

Note that the first part ends, at measure 11, with the chord of the dominant key of G; that the second part ends, at measure 19, with an exactly parallel chord of the tonic key of C; that the third part (and the composition) ends, of course, on the chord of C.

Note that measures 1 and 4 are identical. Also these pairs: 26–27 and 30–31.

Note the parallels between measures 5–6 and 7–8.

Note that measures 8–11 and 16–19 are harmonically identical, though in different keys.

Note that despite the harmonically different content of consecutive measures, there are a few similarities in consecutive measures: left hand is the same in measures 4 and 5; right hand in 8 and 9 and in 16 and 17; left hand in 26 and 27 and in 30 and 31.

Note the pedal-tone (continuously repeated tone) on the dominant G from measures 24 through 31; and the tonic pedal-tone on C from measure 32 through the concluding measure (35).

### 3. Beethoven—Minuet in G

The first part requires the playing of simple right-hand thirds with a legato equal to that with which single notes can be played.

Be sure not to play the ♯♮ , on the third beat of measure 8, as ♫ . This is a mistake easily made because of the many dotted-eighths-plus-sixteenths which precede it.

The trio may be taken slightly faster and more brightly. Variety may be gained by playing each repeated part of the trio half as loud the second time as the first. To make the wide jump from D to G (fourth measure from the end of the trio) as legato as the rest of the piece, spread the hand out as wide as possible when you sound the D; this will bring your fifth finger much nearer the G.

Beware of sentimentality. The minuet was originally a stately dance, though Haydn, Mozart, and Beethoven speeded it up when they poured it into the classical molds of the sonata and the symphony. Keep the three-four dance pulse alive by gentle emphasis on the first beat of each measure.

### Probable fractures:

None, except the jump from D to G already discussed.

### Memory aids:

You find them!

## 4. Grieg—Nocturne, Op. 54, No. 4

Turn back to page 77, where in our discussion of singing tone we took up the first 14 measures of this piece. (Beginning at measure 34, the music parallels the opening 9 measures, taking a different harmonic turning at measure 43 into the Coda, which begins at measure 55.)

Beginning at measure 15, then, hold the right hand's third finger and thumb firmly and rotate the hand for the soft sixteenth notes. As to the trill, try 3–1 as well as the usual 2–3 before making up your mind which to use: select the fingering that gives the maximum smoothness to your trill.

At *Più mosso*, note the change of the time signature to six-eight. Note also the *decrescendo* from *pp* at the beginning (measure 21) of the section to *ppp* in 25; and the *crescendo* beginning at measure 26 (identical, by the way, with measure 25) to the climax of the piece in measures 30 and 31. Be sure to observe the full measure of rest at measure 33; measures 58 and 61 likewise contain nothing but musical silence.

I suggest that you place an X sign at measure 43, to make sure you take the new harmonic turning; otherwise you might find yourself to your dismay in a nocturnal squirrel cage.

I suggest the following device in the last two measures, to obtain the indicated subtle dynamic rise and fall. Play the first chord in the next-to-last measure *pp* with soft pedal down; play the next chord *pp* with soft pedal up; play the final arpeggiated chord with the soft pedal down again, making of the 7 notes a *diminuendo* from *pp* to *ppp*.

**Probable fractures:**

None. The *Più mosso* section, however, is slightly more difficult than the rest of the composition.

**Memory aids:**

The bass line is an identical chromatic downward progression in measures 1–2, 3–4, 34–35, 36–37, and (cut in half) 55–56.

The opening bass notes of measures 5–8 are a different type of chromatic downward progression, repeated in measures 38–41.

The bass-note progressions in measures 12–13 and 46–47 (harmonically identical) are, respectively, B, A, D and E, D, G—think of BAD EDGar and you'll never get the sequence reversed!

Note the concluding Ds of measure 14 which lead to the D which dominates measures 15–17.

Measures 15–17 and 18–20 are harmonically identical, the latter a minor third higher than the former.

Analyze the paired measures 21–22, 23–24, 25–26, and 27–28 for the construction of each pair; and for the similarities and differences of the pairs relative to each other.

Analyze measures 48–54 and discover the simple underlying structure: a series of 7th chords related in measures 48–51 and also related, but in a different way, in measures 51–54.

## 5. Chopin—Mazurka in A minor, Op. 68, No. 2 (posthumous)

This mazurka is perhaps the simplest, and certainly one of the most charming, of Chopin's voluminous contributions to the form.

The tempo indication is *Lento*, but don't drag it.

Observe the occasional accenting of the third beat of the measure, typical of the lilt of this Polish dance.

### Probable fractures:

Measures 3 and 4 of the *Poco più mosso* section and also measures 7 and 8 of this section. Measure 4 is identical with 3 except for the grace notes. Practice measure 4 very, very slowly for many repetitions; increase the speed gradually.

### Memory aids:

The harmonic structure is so simple that memory aids are hardly necessary. The second group of 8 measures in the 16-measure *Poco più mosso*, however, might be scrutinized for the harmonic similarities and differences of the first 4 measures and the last 4.

## 6. Liszt—*Consolation* No. 3

An excellent composition to choose for your "first Liszt piece." It is technically much easier than the hackneyed *Liebestraum* and, in my opinion, better music.

On pages 75–77, we discussed the possibilities for making the melody line sing. The *Consolation* No. 3 is in its entirety a softly singing piece, with a gentle, murmurous accompaniment in the left hand. The right-hand melody is in single notes from the beginning to measure 19, where it is restated in octaves; the octaves should be as legato, and as singing, as the single-note melody. I suggest using the fourth finger on black notes in the octave passages, to facilitate your *legato*. At measure 30, thirds are introduced; these, too, should be *legato*. And all, as Liszt indicated, should be *cantando*.

I think of this composition as having a lesser and a greater climax. The lesser where the A-minor measure 33 modulates, *crescendo*, into the E-major measure 34 —*f* for the whole measure 34, followed by a sudden drop to *ppp* at measure 35. The greater climax begins its *crescendo* in measure 41, continuing all through 42 and reaching its peak on the D-flat chord—*ff*—that opens measure 43; then a drop (gradual this time) to *pp* in the left-hand accompaniment, preparing for the new, lower statement of the theme (let your right hand think of the cello here rather than the violin) at the end of measure 44.

The end should be graded from measure 57 to a mere breath of sound—*ppp*—at the final measure 61. Hold the damper pedal from measure 57 to the end and beyond: at this extreme of the dynamic range the notes merge into sweet, though faintly dissonant, sound. I suggest sounding the final left-hand note of measure 58—D flat—with gentle emphasis, that it may softly but audibly sing its tonic tonality through all the soft notes that follow.

Use the damper pedal lavishly throughout this piece; to hold, full and rich, each deep-bass left-hand whole note; to build up rich overtones in the first three left-hand measures, creating a plush background of blurred sound for the melody as it enters on the last beat of measure 3; to merge and mix the rocking *dolcissimo* thirds in measures 31–32, 39–40, and 57–58; and, as outlined above, to blur the soft conclusion.

Take care throughout that your left hand does not rest too long on the opening note of measures—as, for example, the deep D flat of measure 1: play the next note an eighth rest later—no more but, for that matter, no less.

Note that tie marks in many places indicate that the note on the first beat of the measure is not to be struck but is held over from the preceding measure by the sustaining pedal.

### Rhythmic problems:

The simple two-against-three abounds throughout the piece. This will give you no trouble. There is also much four against three (usually with a silent first note in the four group). If this proves difficult, turn to Appendix B, "How to Solve Problems in Polyrhythm," which begins on page 212.

### Probable fracture:

Measures 41–43.

### Memory aids:

The basic theme is simple:

The top note of the left-hand "handful" at the opening—all through measures 1–8—is F. The right hand's first note, at the end of measure 3, is F.

Measures 3–11 and 19–27 are harmonically identical, but the right hand in measure 11 drops a *major third* from C to A flat, while in measure 28 it drops *two octaves* from C to C.

Note the pedal-tone F through measures 27–33 and

the pedal-tone A through measures 35–40—in each case serving as support for the tonic minor chord, dissonantly for the dominant chord, and then for the tonic major chord. Measures 27–33 and 35–40 are, furthermore, harmonically identical.

The skeleton of the little cadenza in measure 58 is simple: the chord of A major with the passing notes of B and D sharp.

### 7. Debussy—*Danseuses de Delphes*

*Lent et grave* is the fitting tempo indication of this impressionistic music inspired by architectural sculpture. Debussy, according to popular legend, wrote *Danseuses de Delphes* as music to which the three stone maidens atop a pillar from Delphi, which is now in the Louvre, might have danced their archaic, dignified dance. It is a fancy of mine to think that the pillar is a relic from the Delphic Temple of Apollo, in which the oracle was enshrined. It is another fancy of mine to think that the best way to create the mood for playing this composition is to contemplate Keats' *Ode on a Grecian Urn*, particularly the words "slow time" and "Ye soft pipes, play on."

The theme of this first of Debussy's twenty-four preludes is a simple four-note chromatic progression: B flat, B natural, C, C sharp. It is stated in single notes in measures 1 and 2, in octaves in 6 and 7, and in full chords in the 7th and 6th measures from the end. Note that in measures 3 and 4 (following the first statement) and in 8 and 9 (following the second) it is repeated in left-hand octaves with an added chromatic step, D.

Probably bas-relief has nowhere else been so successfully depicted in music. The theme, as first stated, emerges from massive (though soft) surrounding tones; and this treatment continues, elaborated both as to melody and surrounding harmonies.

In measures 1 and 2, play all four of the theme notes with the right hand's second finger, *thinking* them into slight prominence.

Note that measures 4, 9, *10*, and 16, are in four-four time. I italicize 10 because the indicated four beats in it are almost always shortened to three.

Take care—on beat 2 of measures 1 and 2, all three beats of measure 3, and similar places later—not to play the dotted eighth and sixteenth as a double-dotted eighth and a thirty-second. At this slow pace, it is an easy habit to fall into.

From *doux mais en dehors* for four measures, the right-hand octaves must sing as they move slowly and serenely downward while the still softer underlying chords move up.

The tonic chord in the third measure from the end is marked *f;* the repetition of it in the next measure, *pp.* Play the first chord strongly and firmly—Katherine Ruth Heyman, illustrating at the piano during a lesson, said as she played this chord: "Carved in stone!" Play the second chord *pp* by hardly raising the fingers from the keys after the first sounding of the chord. Play the final deep-bass B flat *ppp.*

### Probable fracture:

Measures 16–17, because the time is complicated. Play these measures extremely slowly, counting (loudly, to drill them into your brain) the four beats of measure 16 and the three of 17. Thus: "1 and 2 and 3 and 4 and 1 and 2 and 3." Don't slight the "ands": in these tricky measures they are more important guide posts than the beats themselves. (Note, in this connection, how "and" dominates the three immediately following measures— 18, 19, and 20.)

### Memory aids:

The tonic chord on beat 2 of measure 4 is, on the ensuing "and," taken up intact two octaves, with two notes added in the left hand. Three different positions of the chord of D minor follow immediately. This sequence is repeated in the parallel measures 9 and 10.

In measures 11–12 and 13–14, trace (and remember) the ascent of the bass notes (identical with the top and bottom notes of the right-hand chords). In 11–12, this is a progression from C to C in the key of B flat. What differences in 13–14?

Measure 11 begins with F in the bass, G in the treble; 13 with F again in the bass, C in the treble. The bass F in measure 11 moves up a fifth on the next half-beat to begin its ascent from the triad of C minor; the bass F in 13 moves up a minor third to begin its ascent from the A-flat major triad.

In measures 18, 19, and 20, the chords on the first beat's "and" move chromatically down: A-flat major, G minor, F major.

In measures 21–22, you can help your memory by noting that each left-hand chord that follows a right-hand octave brings the left hand's thumb a major third below the right hand's fifth finger.

Each beat in measures 23 and 24 is a three-note unison, followed on the "and" by a chord. Each unison with its following chord makes a major chord, held in the fundamental position by the left hand and in the first inversion by the right. The sequence of chords here is: B flat, D flat, F, A, C, E. The right hand's melody line is D, F, A, C sharp, E, G sharp.

## 8. Mendelssohn—Scherzo in E minor, Op. 16, No. 2

This scherzo, one of the most delightful of piano compositions, is really a transfigured staccato etude, with legato passages thrown in for good measure. It has a dynamic profile ranging from *pianissimo* to *fortissimo*. Except in its climactic measures, it should be as light as thistledown—an effect best achieved with a light staccato from the wrist.

The opening repeated notes—and the later repetitions of this figure—may be taken by the right hand (fingers 3, 2, 1) or by the right hand (3, 2) aided by the left hand's 3.

For the last eighth note of measure 4, and all of measures 5 and 6, I find it easier (though the passage is written the other way around in the score) to take the repeated Bs with the right-hand thumb, leaving only single notes to be played by the left hand. And the same rearrangement for the last eighth note of measure 12, all of measure 13, and all but the last three eighth notes of measure 14.

Contrast may be obtained by coloring measures 21–22 *p* and 23–24 *pp;* the same with the parallel passage in measures 73–74 and 75–76.

Guard against any tendency, in the left hand's portion of measures 25–27, to relax your touch into *non legato;* keep it a feathery staccato.

On the last half beats of measures 41, 43, 44, and 45 —and the third half beat of measure 46—the left hand has to take the lightning-fast repeated sixteenth notes previously given to the right hand. Don't try too hard or your left hand will tense and balk at these places. Your right hand has been playing similar notes successfully: keeping your left wrist untensed, let your memory of the sound of the right-hand notes guide your left hand. In other words, let your right teach your left.

Up to measure 48, you have been using almost no damper pedal. Begin to use it freely here, and continue through the big climax to measure 69 where the predominating airy quality is resumed. Use it only sparingly again for the remainder.

Be very careful not to hurry the coda, which begins 10 measures before the end. In the 6th and 7th measures before the end, take especial care to pass the right-hand thumb well under the 4th finger; keep your eye on the note—B in each case—toward which your thumb is aiming.

Think of the three measures which usher in the coda —measures 13, 12, and 11 before the end—as a trumpet call. And divide up the trumpet's notes: right hand (3, 2) taking the repeated sixteenths, left hand (4, 2, 1; 4, 2, 1; 2, 1) the quarter notes.

**Probable fractures:**

Measures 6 and 7, because of the right hand's grace note B at the beginning of measure 7. Use the third finger on the B at the end of 6, the second finger on the grace note. *Don't* tighten fingers or wrist here, of all places.

Measure 18, because of the left hand's staccato thirds and fifths.

Measures 25–27, because of the left hand's staccato thirds.

Measures 41, 43, 44, and 45, for left-hand reasons previously referred to.

Measures 53–57, because of the long right-hand *ff* passage in broken chords over the equally *ff* sixteenth-note octaves in the left hand (the latter restating the opening musical theme). I have tried these left-hand octaves with many different touches and finally have settled on a high, stiff * wrist, fifth finger and thumb held firmly in the octave position as they come down *vertically* with motion from elbow. I'm still not satisfied; if you know of a better way to play these octaves, I wish you'd tell me what it is.

The first five measures of the coda. Think of the 3 grace notes and the main note B as a swiftly arpeggiated chord (second inversion of the chord of E ma-

* Yes, stiff—for these few measures.

jor). Practice these measures very, very slowly many, many times.

**Memory aids:**

The left-hand passage in measures 9–11 is the chord of E minor with one passing-note, F sharp. Well, two passing-notes—there's a lone A in measure 11.

Measures 29–34 and the parallel measures 81–86 are, respectively, built on the tonalities of B minor and E minor.

In measures 54–57, think the line of the *top notes* of the broken chords: B, A, G, F sharp, E, C, B, A sharp; followed by the only slightly different B, A, G, F sharp, E, C sharp, A sharp, G. The last three beats of measure 57 are, for the right hand, merely the notes of a broken diminished 7th chord.

Measures 58 and 59, the octaves are built on the diminished 7th chord of B, with passing notes—or rather passing octaves.

The coda, with passing notes, is constructed in one piece out of the chord of E major.

## 9. Debussy—*Clair de lune*

Debussy's *Suite bergamasque* was published in June of 1905. Some commentators hold that *Clair de lune*, the third in the set, was entitled *Promenade sentimentale* in an earlier version of the suite. True or untrue, this is a useful interpretative idea. If untrue, the thought should be used just the same, tender moonlight and the tender sentiment being such closely related phenomena.

Every Debussy composition, no matter how much it may seem like an exquisitely melodious fog of sound, is as vertebrate as any classic. Remember this especially in the opening nine measures of *Clair de lune*, which are lamentably often played as though they were not only dreamy but spineless. They have a spine, as does the rest of the piece. This is its shape: $\frac{9}{8}$. Let your opening be dreamy, moonlit, love-filled, *rubato*, and (Debussy's own direction) *très expressif*—but first detect its spinal column. A good way to do this is the prosaic one of playing, and counting (every beat), these nine measures many times and *loudly*. Later will be time enough for musical practice.

Use throughout, as nearly as you can achieve it, Godowsky's "clinging" touch (see pages 99–100).

Every time I take up *Clair de lune* for restudy, I am confronted by this warning, in my own handwriting: "Halt! Do you *know* the similarities and differences of A and B?"

A is 6 measures, 9 through 14; B is 4 measures, from

the 14th-from-last through the 11th-from-last. Mark off these measures and study them until you can see them in your sleep. Note how B's third measure has the same melody as A's third, but, in the bass, a harmonic change, similar to (but not identical with) the bass in A's fifth measure. Note the resemblances, and differences, of A's sixth measure and B's fourth.

Be sure to hold all soprano notes their full indicated time, as: the dotted half note C in measure 4 held over to an eighth note C in 5; the quarter note F in measure 6 held over to an eighth note F in 7; the dotted quarter note F in 11 held over to an eighth note F in 12—and all similar places, of which there are many. Don't cut them short.

The lesser climax is at measure 25, the greater at 41. Think, if the idea appeals to you, of full moonlight breaking through in all its silver glory at measure 25; and, at measure 41 (the only *forte* in the piece), think of the passionate kiss for which this promenade was undertaken in the first place.

Be sure your pedal holds all the left hand's dotted half notes from the 22nd-from-last measure for the next eight measures.

In my opinion, the C flat in the 14th-from-last measure is the most significant note in the whole composition. If you agree, make it sound significant.

The treble A flat taken by the left hand in the 8th-from-last measure has an aching beauty.

### Probable fractures:

Measures 41 and 42, already discussed in detail as an illustrative fracture (turn back to pages 60–64).

It would also be well to isolate for intensive practicing the left hand's passages in measures 29–30 and 45–46 and the right hand's in measures 36–39.

### Memory aids:

Mastering A and B, as discussed earlier, is not only a memory aid but an essential preliminary to secure memory of the entire piece.

If you compare measures 5 and 7 carefully, your memory will benefit.

Line of deep-bass octaves in measures 18–23.

The three groups of left-hand notes in measure 36 are successive inversions of the same broken chord. In the right hand, the second group is an inversion of the broken chord of the first group, but the third group differs—how?

Compare the right hand of the 22nd-from-last measure through the 8th-from-last measure, with the right hand of the opening 14 measures.

## 10. Chopin—Nocturne in F sharp, Op. 15, No. 2

In this Nocturne, which is one of the finest compositions in the whole range of piano literature, your playing must be a composite of these elements: a singing tone, extreme delicacy of touch where needed, dynamic power at the climax.

For the singing tone—which is required everywhere but in the dramatic middle section—reread the passage on Godowsky's clinging touch (pages 99–100) and *think* your right hand into employing its velvet magic. Soften your left hand relative to your right: your right will then sing more clearly and roundly.

In measure three, the five-against-two is simply solved by placing the left hand's second note exactly between the right hand's third and fourth notes.

Don't drag the tempo anywhere. Note that the tempo indication is not *Largo*, as most amateurs play this piece, but *Larghetto*. And, while keeping your melody line flexible, don't employ too much *rubato*. Which means: don't oversentimentalize.

Technically, except for the two cadenzalike right-hand passages which we will take up in detail in a moment, the middle section—marked *doppio movimento*—is the most difficult. In the first place, be sure to *doppio* the *movimento*. Too often, this section is taken only slightly faster than the preceding and following sections: it should, of course, be twice as fast. As to the five-against-two here, you have already solved this simple polyrhythmic problem in measure 3 of the piece: now merely play it in faster tempo. *Warning:* the entire section is not in five-against-two—only the first eight measures. At measure nine of this section there is a subtle rhythmic change—subtle because the character of the section (mounting excitement) is not changed by the rhythmic change: it is merely intensified. I think of the climax coming at the E-natural right-hand octave (measure 16 of the doubled tempo)—it is the high note toward which all the preceding 16 measures have been building. It should be also the dynamic high point of the composition: *ff*.

In the coda—last five measures—be careful not to let the rococo passage-work of the right hand, or the four thick repeated F-sharp chords in the left, betray you into loudness. These measures are a *diminuendo* from *pp* to *ppp*. A more characterful final dying-away sound will result if your right hand emphasizes ever so slightly the last note (C sharp) in the next-to-last measure: it will then sing on softly through the accumulated preceding tones and overtones and the framing treble A sharp and bass F sharp which follow.

**Probable fractures:**

The entire *doppio movimento* section will probably require more practice than the rest of the piece, except,

Measure 11 and the even more florid 12th-from-the-last measure. These measures (below) are also poly-rhythmic problems. They are, respectively, 30 against 4 and 40 against 4. At first blush, they would seem to require treatment by Katherine Ruth Heyman's mathematically accurate method of solving problems in

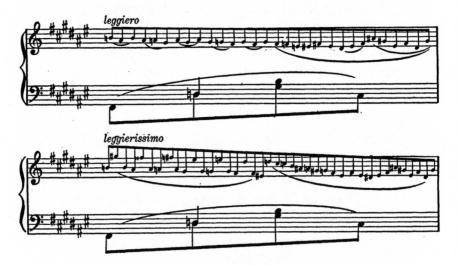

polyrhythm (Appendix B). Actually, however, these measures are a special case in polyrhythm. By tradition, they are played with the right hand markedly retarding its final notes. Therefore they must be solved in a different way.

I divide the notes up between the hands as follows, keeping the left hand going at the same tempo and equal spacing of notes it has held from the outset of the piece:

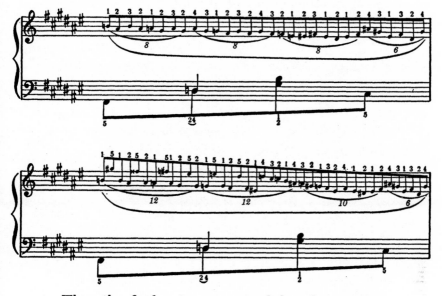

Thus the final notes are retarded and a musical parallel is made between the two passages by retarding the same six notes in each case. This requires the right hand to play even more swiftly in the second passage, for it must there play 12, 12, and 10 notes to the left hand's eighth notes, as against 8, 8, and 8 in the first passage. The fingering shown here is Joseffy's, with one

or two changes which suit my hand better. Play these
delicate right-hand passages with the hand close to the
keys, the fingers moving lightly, the wrist (especially
in the second passage) loose. Note the *decrescendo* sign
which precedes each passage: it is my suggestion that
you play both passages *una corda*.

### Memory aids:

Comparing the opening of the composition with the
final 14 measures, how are these final measures shortened
by elision?

In measures 22 and 23, the left hand has four mne-
monically helpful A-sharp octaves.

The right hand's second and third fingers, in measures 25–26 and 29–30, play repetitively identical notes.

Note the relation of the right-hand octave line in
measures 25–28 and 29–32. In which later measures is
this repeated in a different tonality?

Five left-hand C-sharp octaves in measures 39–41.

The entire coda is built on the tonic chord of F sharp
with only two passing notes, D sharp and B. This could
be called the Black Key Coda, but for the white-sheep
B.

———

I finished memorizing the F-sharp Nocturne in the

village of Montauk. And thereby hangs a strange tale.

My wife and I took a January vacation last year: a week in Montauk, at the tip of Long Island. Montauk and its dunes, during the off-season, have a bleak, ocean-chilled charm which I won't try to describe. We lived comfortably in a rented room in the home of Peter Le Blanc, a French-Canadian clam fisherman.

As you may have divined earlier in these pages, I don't like to miss my daily hour at the piano. I will, in fact, go to considerable lengths to avoid missing it. Down at Montauk I went to the length of discovering, by dint of asking all over town, that there was an upright piano in the Montauk Community Church which might perhaps be practiced upon. The minister was kind enough to tell me I could use the piano at any time that church wasn't in session.

On the last day of this midwinter idyl, the sexton of the church dropped in where I was practicing, listened for a while, and said: "How do you find her?"

"Excellent," I said. "Good tone, even register, and pedals that work like a charm."

The sexton—a gray-haired, affable gentleman—nodded to indicate that he knew she was excellent before I told him.

"But what are those whitish streaks on the case?" I asked.

"Those," said the sexton, "are the only marks of her adventure which I couldn't eradicate."

"Her adventure—?"

"That piano was in the 1938 hurricane," said the sexton, "and I mean she was *in* it! The house which was her former home, down the shore here a piece, was turned upside down, inside out, and hasn't been seen since. As for the piano, she floated a couple of miles out to sea and then rode back on the crest of the monster tidal wave, as neat as a surfboard rider. She beached not ten yards from where she set sail."

I looked from him to the piano and back.

"But how on earth did she get here?" I asked.

"I'm coming to that," said the sexton. "When the lady who owned the house got down here from New York next day and saw what had happened, she told me we could have the piano for the Community Church if I could salvage it. She knew we needed one here. I took her up on the offer before she finished making it, and trucked the piano over here the selfsame day. And then I put in six solid weeks of work on her. Ten hours a day including the Sabbath, though I guess the Lord will forgive me in view of the circumstances. I rubbed every speck of rust off every wire. I sandpapered all the swollen wood. I tightened every loose screw. I massaged the felt on every hammer."

"You must have been a piano craftsman by trade once," I said, "or you couldn't have done all that!"

"I was not," said the sexton. "But forty years ago I drove a delivery wagon for a piano company in East St. Louis and I sometimes watched the workmen. I remembered what I saw, that's all. Well, when I got her all spruced up I had a tuner down from East Hampton. And we've been using her ever since as much as any piano is ever used. Choir rehearsal, Sunday school, besides Tuesday nights when a violinist and cellist get together with our organist as pianist and play trios. Now and then I sit down at her myself and play what I can remember; I studied piano when I was a boy and I've always been sorry I gave it up."

He paused.

"Not to mention Saturday nights in summer," he said, "when we truck her down to the village green for a community sing."

"Well," I said, "you certainly did a fine job of fixing her up!"

The sexton came over and stroked the piano's case lovingly.

"I think I did," he said. "In view of what I had to take out of her first."

"What did you take out?"

"Three buckets of sand," said the sexton, "some rocks

as big as baseballs, twenty yards of seaweed, two striped bass, and a weakfish."

With such a spirit abroad in the land, fellow amateurs, I submit that the piano is here to stay.

# Appendix A

Some Suggestions about Selecting a Teacher, a
Piano, Books of Music, and Books on Music

### Selecting a Teacher

IF YOU have never had piano lessons but have come to
a decision to take up the study of this king of musical
instruments, be sure to select a good teacher. One way to
go about this is to ask your local music dealer to give
you a few names of teachers who work well with adult
beginners. Another way is to get in touch with your
local music teachers' organization, if there is one. Still
another way is to write to *Keyboard*, the magazine for
piano teachers (1346 Chapel Street, New Haven,
Conn.); its obliging editor, Mr. Ian Mininberg, will
put you in touch with a good piano teacher if there is
one in your vicinity. There probably is, for there are
some 100,000 teachers of piano in the United States,
and the number, like the number of pianos and piano
students, is growing all the time.

If you have studied the piano in the past and would

like to take it up again, be sure (I repeat) to select a good teacher. At any stage of pianistic development short of the status of virtuoso, a good teacher will spur your progress.

As to the frequency of lessons, twice a week for a beginner is not too often. But adults making a hobby of piano study don't always have that much time available. One lesson a week will serve if it is impossible to find time for two. After passing the elementary stage, once a week will be quite often enough for adult students.

Prices vary with individual teachers, but some music teachers' organizations set a minimum of one or two dollars per lesson. Five dollars per lesson, after passing the elementary stage, may be considered a fair average price.

## Selecting a Piano

I would like to explode the myth that piano study, if you don't already own a piano, is something of a luxury hobby by reason of the necessity of buying or renting an instrument.

Recently, passing the Edward W. Powers Piano Company on West Fifty-seventh Street in New York, I saw a sign on the showroom window which read: PRACTICE PIANO FOR SALE—$35. I went in and asked if I could see this piano. I was taken to an upright of the York make, and I discovered that its keys were even and firm, its tone round, and its pedals in good working order. "We've got a hundred others like it," said the salesman. If this surprises you, the answer is that upright pianos *of the old large type* have become, through the tremendous popularity of the new, smaller, spinet-size uprights, a drug on the used-piano market.

If, at the moment, your purse is lean but your desire to get a piano strong, look into the used-upright market in your locality. You will probably discover some amazing bargains in pianos that are—like the $35 piano in the Powers showrooms—serviceable and satisfactory for practicing (and for playing) purposes.

Look into the whole used-piano market while you're at it. I once stumbled upon a Steinway concert grand, getting on in years but mellow in tone and action, which was offered for $100. Nothing but lack of room at my home (and lack of the necessary funds) prevented me from taking it on the spot. When a concert grand— they're nine feet long, you know—gets into the used-piano market, they are white elephants. Why? Because most homes, in these days of vertical life, can no more accommodate a nine-foot piano than a mastodon. But occasionally an unusually large living room and a lover of piano music find each other; then if the music lover finds a used concert grand—!

Small grands of good quality may be bought today,

new, for as little as $200. So can the new spinet-size uprights. You can buy a piano through Sears, Roebuck, by mail order, if you live in the country—or if you live in a city, for that matter.

Pianos may be rented for as low as $3 a month for an upright to as high as $50 a month for a fine grand. You'll also have to pay cartage charges. Renting a piano is not advisable unless the period for which you want it is short. My beloved Steinway, a "Rebuilt" (by the Steinway Company) Model B, required installment payments of about $30 a month; had I rented it, the cost would have been $50 a month, plus cartage charges to and from my home to the tune of $12 a trip.

Today it is possible to buy a new Steinway spinet-size upright piano for $495; the somewhat larger Steinway Pianino is $585; the Steinway Baby Grands run from $985 to $1,275; and the other Steinway grands designed for home use ascend from this price level to as high as $2,175.

The best advice you can follow, of course, is to call on your local piano dealer.

### BOOKS OF MUSIC

Albums of music recommended for browsing, sight-reading, and general enjoyment:

# General

*The American Home Music Album.* This jumbo volume is called by its publishers the largest collection of music in the world. Its 1,000 pages contain 125 piano pieces (classical, romantic, modern, light, sacred, operatic) and 225 songs of various kinds. It is published by Appleton-Century and sells for $5.

# Piano

*60 Progressive Piano Pieces You Like to Play.* Schirmer. $1.

*59 Piano Solos You Like to Play.* Schirmer. $1.

*51 Piano Pieces from the Modern Repertoire.* Schirmer. $1.

*World's Greatest Composers Album* (piano compositions by Brahms, Liszt, Schumann, Beethoven, and so on). Carl Fischer. 50¢.

*Piano Music.* Willis Music Company. $1.

*Masterpieces of Piano Music.* Mumil Publishing Co. Called by its publishers the world's largest collection of standard piano music—over 200 pieces. $2.

*Mammoth Collection of Famous Piano Music.* Robbins. $1.

*Everybody's Favorite Album of Selected Piano Music.* Amsco. $1.

*Everybody's Favorite Album of Modern Piano Music.* Amsco. $1.

*Piano Music for the Leisure Hour.* Longmans, Green. $1.50.

*Piano Pieces the Whole World Plays.* Appleton-Century. $1.25.

*Modern Piano Pieces the Whole World Plays.* Appleton-Century. 75¢.

---

(easy) *Piano Pieces for Children.* Amsco. $1.

## Violin and piano

*Twelve Classics for Violin and Piano.* Edited by Louis J. Bostelmann. Schirmer. 75¢.

*Violin and Piano Music.* Willis. $1.

*Everybody's Favorite Violin Pieces.* Amsco. $1.

*Violin Music the Whole World Plays.* Willis. 75¢.

*Violin Pieces the Whole World Plays.* Appleton-Century. $2.

*Charming Airs and Old Dance Forms.* Fifteen compositions for violin and piano by old masters. Fischer. $1.

*Elman Favorite Encores.* Edited by Mischa Elman. Fischer. $1.75.

*Fritz Kreisler Favorite Encore Folio.* Edited by Fritz Kreisler. Fischer. $1.75.

*New Favorite Encore Folio.* Edited by Jascha Heifetz. Fischer. $2.

(difficult) *Standard Violin Album.* 36 concert numbers for advanced players. Fischer. $1.

## Vocal

*Songs Children Love to Sing.* Appleton-Century. 75¢.
*Songs the Whole World Sings.* Appleton-Century. 75¢.
*Everybody's Favorite Songs.* Amsco. $1.
*Ballads the Whole World Sings.* Appleton-Century. 75¢.
*Songs of Stephen Foster.* Harcourt, Brace. $2.
*Songs of the Sunny South.* Appleton-Century. 75¢.

### BOOKS ON MUSIC

Below are listed some of the outstanding books on the appreciation, history, and analysis of music:

*Great Pianists on Piano Playing.* James Francis Cooke. Presser. $2.25.
*Piano Playing with Piano Questions Answered.* Josef Hofmann. Presser. $2.
*The Piano—Its History, Makers, Players, and Music.* Albert E. Wier. Longmans, Green. $3.50.
*Approach to Music.* Lawrence Abbott. Farrar and Rinehart. $2.50.
*Men and Women Who Make Music.* David Ewen. Thomas Y. Crowell. $3.50.
*You Can Enjoy Music.* Helen L. Kaufman. Reynal and Hitchcock. $2.
*Musical Questions and Quizzes—a Digest of Information*

*About Music.* Marion Bauer. G. P. Putnam's Sons. $2.

*Music Appreciation.* Percy Scholes. Witmark. $4.

*Men of Music.* Wallace Brockway and Herbert Weinstock. Simon and Schuster. $3.75.

*How to Understand Music.* Oscar Thompson. Dial. $1.29.

*How Music Grew.* Marion Bauer and Ethel Peyser. Putnam. $4.50.

*The Story of Music.* Paul Bekker. Norton. $3.50.

*The Well-Tempered Listener.* Deems Taylor. Simon and Schuster. $2.50.

*Music—a Science and an Art.* John Redfield. Tudor. $1.29.

*A Musical Companion.* Edited by John Erskine. Knopf. $3.

*The Art of Enjoying Music.* Sigmund Spaeth. Garden City Publishing Co. $1.39.

*The Gist of Music.* George A. Wedge. Schirmer. $2.50.

*The Magic World of Music.* Olga Samaroff-Stokowski. Norton. $2.50.

*The Book of Musical Knowledge—the History, Technique, and Appreciation of Music, Together with Lives of the Great Composers.* Houghton Mifflin. $1.89.

*Music in History.* McKenny and Anderson. American Book Co. $4.50.

*Encyclopedia of Music and Musicians.* Parkhurst and de Bekker. Crown. $2.75.

*New Encyclopedia of Music and Musicians.* Waldo Selden Pratt. Macmillan. $3.50.

*The International Cyclopedia of Music and Musicians.* Edited by Oscar Thompson. Dodd, Mead. $12.50.

*The History of Music.* Waldo Selden Pratt. Schirmer. $3.

*Complete History of Music.* W. J. Baltzell. Presser. $2.25.

*History of Musical Thought.* Donald N. Ferguson. Crofts. $5.

*The Oxford Companion to Music.* Percy Scholes. Oxford University Press. $7.

*Baker's Biographical Dictionary of Musicians.* Schirmer. $6.

# Appendix B

## How to Solve Problems in Polyrhythm

DURING the early stages of piano study, we all come to polyrhythm. The simplest kind, and the easiest to play, is two notes against three. A familiar example of two against three is the following passage, measures 49 and 50 from the first section of the first movement of Mozart's Sonata in F (Köchel listing 300K):

(This passage, in C the first time, is repeated, in F and with the right hand in octaves, in the second section of the movement.)

Two against three usually seems difficult at first. Most teachers tell their pupils to solve it by one of two methods. A method which often brings success quickly is as follows:

*Step 1.* Make a mental note of the fact that in the final, correct execution of two against three, the second note of the two-group is played *exactly between* the second and third notes of the three-group. Never mind why this is so; just make a mental note of it.

*Step 2.* Play the two-groups alone with the right hand, strongly counting (up to the proper tempo of the piece) one beat to a group. Play, thus, the two measures complete and the first note of the third measure. Do this many times.

*Step 3.* Play the three-groups alone with the left hand, counting one beat to a group as before. Now you'll be playing three notes to a beat instead of two. Be sure your counted beats are the same in both steps; use a metronome, if you have one, to ensure this. Finish each repetition, as in Step 2, on the first note of the third measure.

*Step 4.* Alternate the duple and triple rhythms by doing Steps 2 and 3 many times.

*Step 5.* Put the hands together, counting your three beats to a measure with especial firmness. If nothing results at first except a jumble, go back to Steps 2 and 3 and do them many times again. Then put the hands together again. Sooner or later, the hands will suddenly "go" together. You will be playing two against three accurately. Finally you will be able to play it with the greatest of ease, your hands taking their two-groups and three-groups per beat automatically; you'll be able to listen to the two-groups without disturbing the rhythm of the three-groups; and vice versa. You will have solved two against three and will be able to apply it anywhere, in fast or slow tempo, with the two-groups and three-groups in the right hand or the left hand.

This method requires acquiring a knack. Sometimes the knack is slow in coming, or doesn't come. There is another method. This:

*Step 1.* Play the passage through at a funereally slow pace, placing, with finicking accuracy, the second note of each two-group exactly between the second and third notes of each three-group.

*Step 2.* As soon as you can do this in extreme slow motion, begin to increase the tempo. At each faster tempo, do many repetitions. Finally, you will be able to play the passage correctly up to tempo.

Though this second method consists of only two steps, it usually takes longer than the first method.

Either method solves two against three. And an extension of either method will solve any polyrhythmic problem when a two-group is one factor—as two against 5, 7, 9, or any other odd number. (Two against an even number is not, of course, a polyrhythmic problem.) In two against five, place the second note of the two-group exactly between the third and fourth note of the five-group. In two against seven, between the fourth and fifth notes of the seven-group. And so on, for mathematical reasons we'll come to in a moment. No other methods than those just outlined need ever be used for two against any odd number.

But many teachers (and artists) use the first of these two methods for three against four, five against three, seven against six, and so on: the different groups are taken separately, the beats counted firmly, and finally the groups are put together. This is inadequate, however, unless a two-group is one factor. In more complicated problems, the adjustment to each other of the conflicting rhythmic groups is never so simple; solving them by counting from beat to beat means muddling through, probably inaccurately and certainly with no understanding of the relatively simple mathematics of the problems. It usually results in nervous dread of the passages, a dread based on the knowledge that they have been solved only in a superficial, slapdash way. How often a piano student drops a piece of fine music in despair because he "just can't play" its polyrhythmic passages. Or, worse, how often a student does play such a piece, making hash of these passages and unsettling both himself and his listeners.

Readers of this book are the fortunate beneficiaries of Katherine Ruth Heyman's kind permission to present here her method of solving problems in polyrhythm, with which she masters, with scientific accuracy, the polyrhythmic problems in the standard repertoire and the tremendous polyrhythmic problems found in the works of Scriabin. It is the only correct method to use for polyrhythm. It gives such absolute mastery that the artistry of *tempo rubato* may be used in whatever degree desired in the passages so mastered, much as gently undulating water molds the images which it reflects. As applied by Miss Heyman, it is a facet of the highest art.

The first step in learning this method is to drop blind acceptance of the fact that in two against three the second note of the two-group is played exactly between the second and third notes of the three-group. Ask, instead, why this is so. Let us lift a two-against-three group out of its context in the previous Mozart example, together with the first note of the next group:

What is the lowest common denominator of two and three? Six.

Write out the numbers from 1 to 6, adding the "1" of the next group:

|1 2 3 4 5 6|1

Now place marks to show how, in the example chosen (which has the two-group in the right hand and the three-group in the left), the groups divide into six:

$$\overline{|1 \; 2 \; \overline{3} \; \overline{4} \; 5 \; 6|1}$$

Now you know, mathematically, why two against three is played as it is.

Figure out, similarly, two against five. Against seven.

Two against an odd number of notes need never be solved by Miss Heyman's method, so let us go on to three against four, illustrating again with a familiar example—from measure 18 of Chopin's Nocturne in E flat, Op. 9, No. 2:

The lowest common denominator of 3 and 4 is 12, so the group is broken down into its numerical skeleton thus:

$$\left|\overline{1}\ 2\ 3\ \overline{4}\ \underline{5}\ 6\ \overline{7}\ 8\ \underline{9}\ \overline{10}\ 11\ 12\right|\overline{1}$$

You can see at a glance that no such easy direction as "play this note exactly between these two notes" can apply here. Notes are played between other notes, but not exactly between: there are now minute differences in timing.

We are already well into Miss Heyman's method. The next step is to note that the three-group will be the guiding group here, because it is a part of the steady left-hand accompaniment (eighth notes grouped in threes) of the entire piece. Therefore let us renumber so that in counting aloud we may emphasize the three-group rather than the four-group:

$$\left|\overline{1}\ 2\ 3\ \overline{4}\ \underline{2}\ \overline{2}\ \overline{3}\ 4\ 3\ \overline{2}\ 3\ 4\right|\overline{1}$$

(You know how chamber-music players, counting their long rests of 14 or 21 or 35 measures, count thus: "Nine two three four, ten two three four, eleven two three four—" and so on.)

—*218*—

Now count *very slowly*—"One two three four, two
two three four, three two three four, one"—patting
your left hand on the piano at the indicated 1, 2, and
3, and on the 1 of the next group. Do this many times.

Count again in the same way, patting your right
hand on the indicated 1, 4, 3, 2, and on the 1 of the next
group. It will be harder to do than the left hand was, for
the numbers won't help you by running consecutively.
Do this many times.

Now, continuing to count aloud very slowly, put the
hands together, patting the three-group and the four-
group against each other. Do this many times and take
especial care that you master it completely at this slow
pace, for you are now accurately patting three against
four.

Increase the tempo of your counting somewhat. Do
many repetitions at each faster pace.

Now pat without counting, listening very carefully
to the sound of the rhythm of three against four. It will
sound, roughly, like *dum tah-dum dum t'dum.*

It will now be easy to pat out *dum tah-dum dum
t'dum* faster and faster (without counting) until you
have reached the indicated tempo of the piece—in this
case *andante.*

When you can pat the hands to this rhythm at any
pace you choose (testing occasionally by counting, to

make sure you maintain absolute accuracy) and when you can pat the hands to this rhythm so unconsciously that it will continue while your mind (purposely) wanders—then you are ready to substitute the bass notes of the passage for your left-hand pats and the treble notes for the right-hand pats.

You will be playing three against four with absolute accuracy, and, once this is achieved in strict time, you can, on this rock-solid rhythmic foundation, mold the passage into whatever Chopinesque flexibility your musical instinct tells you to employ.

That is an example of uncomplicated three against four. For an example of more complex three against four, see the analysis of the opening measure of Scriabin's *Flammes sombres*, which begins on page 223.

Four against five is a good polyrhythmical problem to consider next. If you don't have an example of it in your active repertoire, you'll find four solid measures of four against five beginning with the 7th measure from the end of Rachmaninoff's Prelude in G (Op. 32, No. 5). Four against five is written out numerically thus:

1 2 3 4 5 6 7 8 9 10 11 12 13 14 15 16 17 18 19 20 1,

which, as the five-group is the predominating rhythmic group in this composition, we will renumber this way:

| 1 2 3 4 2̄ 2̄ 3 4 3 2̄ 3 4 4 2 3 4̄ 5 2 3 4 | 1̄ |

You will have no rhythmical difficulty at all with these four measures if you use this method; you can concentrate on mastering the double thirds in the right hand.

It will be excellent practice in applying Miss Heyman's method if, when you study the Chopin Nocturne, Op. 72, No. 1, you use it to solve—in the piece's two fractures (turn back to pages 58–59)—the successive problems of 8 against 3, 10 against 3, and 11 against 3 which occur in this fracture. The least common denominators are, respectively, 24, 30, and 33.

*Languidamente è molto rubato*

I have heard a dozen pianists play Charles T. Griffes' lovely composition, *The White Peacock*, in concert. This piece opens with a 7 against 3 which is repeated in the next measure (above). All the dozen pianists used the by-guess-and-by-God method which serves well enough for 2 against 3; and the result was a dozen different rhythms for the opening—all, in greater or less degree, wrong.

When Miss Heyman plays this piece, it is not only hauntingly beautiful and hauntingly evocative of a white peacock strolling languidly on a perfect lawn in the June sun—the opening is also rhythmically accurate and exquisitely molded. And so are the examples of 3 against 10, and the two examples of 2 against 5, which occur in measure 43 as the piece approaches its climax:

The two 2-against-5 examples, as you already know, are the easiest to solve of all *The White Peacock*'s poly-rhythmic problems.

As a final example, I want to take up another instance of 3 against 4. As we saw in the example from Chopin's E-flat Nocturne, 3 against 4, when uncomplicated, is not difficult to solve. The example which follows is com-plicated, however, because it is not, as all the other examples previously shown are, the rhythmic problem in simple outline. Solving it will show you how to solve other problems which are not a simple outline state-ment of polyrhythm. It is from Scriabin's dark, excit-ing composition, *Flammes sombres*—the opening meas-ure (with which the 2nd, 3rd, 48th, 49th, and 50th measures of the piece are rhythmically identical):

(Actually, this should be called a problem in poly-metric, for Scriabin wrote the treble in $\frac{6}{8}$ time and the bass in $\frac{2}{4}$. But that, like the difference between C flat and B, is an apparent, not a real, difference.)

First, write out the numerical skeleton:

$$\bar{1}\ 2\ 3\ \bar{4}\ \bar{5}\ 6\ 7\ \bar{8}\ \bar{9}\ 10\ 11\ 12\ \bar{1}$$

The three-group is the predominating rhythmic unit throughout the composition, so renumber the skeleton accordingly:

$$\bar{1}\ 2\ 3\ 4\ \bar{2}\ 2\ 3\ 4\ \bar{3}\ 2\ 3\ 4\ \bar{1}$$

Forgetting the notes for a while, pat this rhythm until you can pat it up to the tempo of the piece (which begins *Avec une grâce dolente*, or roughly, I would say, *allegretto*).

Now omit the first left-hand pat. Pat it the new way until it becomes automatically accurate.

Substitute for the pats the notes of the first half measure, omitting the right hand's A in the arpeggiated major tenth.

When you can play the half measure in this way with monotonous unconscious accuracy, insert the right hand's A, playing it like a grace note before the beat. Your rhythmic foundation will be so secure now that you won't need to worry about just where this grace note is to be played relative to the other notes. Simply insert it just before the **D** flat, as you would insert a grace note in any passage.

Having mastered the first half measure, you'll have no difficulty mastering the second half, which (though it is complicated like the first in having a sixteenth rest instead of a sixteenth note to open the four-group) has no grace note to complicate it further.

The way to solve polyrhythmic problems which are thus complicated by the composer is: strip off the complicating elements and learn the underlying rhythmic structure; put the complicating elements back in place.

*A generality to remember in all polyrhythmic work: the voice with the larger number of notes always plays the first note after the opening simultaneous notes of both voices.*

# Appendix C

### Ensemble Playing

*Hausmusik* is more widely enjoyed in America now than it was a few decades ago. But there should be far, far more of it. In this chapter I am going to discuss various kinds of *Hausmusik* and present concrete suggestions for (*a*) forming groups with yourself at the piano as nucleus and (*b*) obtaining musical materials to work with.

### Vocal

Gather-around-the-piano songs such as *Old Black Joe, Little Brown Jug, Funiculi Funicula, Carry Me Back to Old Virginny,* and *Polly Wolly Doodle* make a good starting point. Everybody likes to sing them and the piano accompaniments are not difficult; anybody who can play hymns can play community songs. They are required singing when evenings around the flowing bowl become mornings around same. Nobody has a better time than the accompanist, who is permitted by tradition to sing at the top of his lungs himself. Bob Simon, music critic of *The New Yorker*, gave this lusty, deathless form of vocal music an immortal name—barber-Chopin—and volumes chockful of these classics are available for a song. The C. C. Birchard Company of Boston sells *Twice 55 Plus Community Songs*, which contains 175 songs, for fifteen cents. For a quarter you can get Carl Fischer's *Living Songs*, Hall & McCreary's *Songs We Sing*, Robbins Music Corporation's *America Sings*, Birchard's *Singing America*, and Feist's *Merrily We Sing*. Hall & McCreary also put out, for thirty cents, the *New American Song Book*. These volumes are all first-rate for the purpose.

Where community songs leave off and folk songs begin is a nebulous boundary. I'll beg the question by just mentioning some folk-song volumes of acknowledged excellence: *The Universal Folk Songster*, Schirmer, thirty cents; *Songs of the Americas*, also Schirmer, seventy-five cents. Carl Sandburg's great (and fat) *The American Songbag*, originally published by Harcourt, Brace at $7.50, is now available at $1.98. The pianistically interesting *Treasury of American Song* is put out by Howell, Soskin for five dollars; this collection is edited by Olin Downes, music critic of *The New York Times*, and each song (there are 150 of them, arranged in historical sequences) has a special piano arrangement—of medium difficulty—by Elie Siegmeister.

Christmas carols are a joy to sing, especially in December; at fifty cents, Schirmer has a volume entitled *Christmas Carols from Many Countries,* and, at the same price, Willis has one called *Fifty Christmas Carols of All Nations.* Hendrik van Loon and Grace Castagnetta have collaborated on Simon & Schuster's volume, *Christmas Carols,* which is slender in girth but rich in content: 20 favorite carols selected by Dr. van Loon, each with an easy piano accompaniment written by Miss Castagnetta ($2).

Suggestions about accompanying such group songs needn't go further than the advice to play strongly, accurately, and above all with a solid rhythm. The singers will look to you especially for leadership in rhythm.

Other volumes of group songs are listed in Appendix A.

Accompanying solo songs by the great composers is another matter. Often the accompaniments are not of great technical difficulty, but always—as in the case of piano accompaniments to serious instrumental music such as violin and cello compositions—the accompanist must play accurately, musically, with due regard to his function as accompanist rather than soloist, and with one ear always alertly listening to the soloist. The accompanist must both lead and follow. Experience is the best educator for accompanying.

For vocal repertoire, I refer you to Schirmer's huge catalogs, "Secular Vocal Music" and "Sacred Vocal Music." First-rate solo songs, with piano accompaniments which are not too difficult, are: Mozart's *Alleluia*, Handel's *Where E'er You Walk*, Bach's *My Heart Ever Faithful*, Grieg's *Ich Liebe Dich*.

One of the most interesting ventures open to an amateur pianist who lives in a musical community is to organize a choral group—for evenings of music at home which perhaps can be developed to the point where public concerts can be given. My sister, Lucy E. Cooke, a graduate of the Eastman School of Music, has for the last eight years directed annual concerts in Cooperstown, N. Y., of the Cooperstown Glee Club of fifty voices, which she founded in 1934. She has provided me with expert opinion on the structure and repertoire of amateur choral groups. Of course, the voice combinations depend on what is available in your community. There can be duos, trios, quartets, quintets, sextets, and so on; and there is more or less extensive literature for each combination (see the Schirmer catalogs). If you are able to develop your group to the point of a mixed chorus of twenty-five, a good balance would be ten sopranos, six altos, four tenors, and five basses. For fifty voices, the ideal set-up would be twenty sopranos, fifteen altos, six tenors, and nine basses. If, through the years, you should bring your choral group to the point of giving concerts, bear in mind the following suggestions of my sister, whose skill in program-making has been praised by such authorities as Samuel Richards Gaines, the American composer, and Dr. Elmer A. Tidmarsh, director of music at Union College:

*Group One.* Bach, Handel, or other early music. Always sacred music.

*Group Two.* An English group is advisable.

*Group Three.* A Russian group.

*Group Four.* The program's climactic number should be in this group.

INTERMISSION

*Group Five.* Not too heavy. Negro spirituals may well be used here.

*Group Six.* This a good place for an American group.

*Group Seven.* End with something inspiring and, if possible, familiar.

General suggestions: Don't have your groups, or your concert, too long. Don't use mediocre material. Mix *a cappella* (unaccompanied) numbers with both sacred and secular music. It is also wise to include humorous songs occasionally, such as "The Pedlar" by Ernest A. Dicks, "Spinning Top" by Rimsky-Korsakoff, and "Jabberwocky" by Henry Jacobsen.

## Instrumental

The amateur pianist bent on extracting the maximum enjoyment from his increasing skill is fortunate if he has a friend who plays the violin, cello, viola, flute, clarinet, or some other solo instrument.

Albums of violin-and-piano music are especially useful when the skill of either performer is in the elementary or intermediate stage. I recommend as an opening wedge the *Violinist's First Solo Album*, volumes I and II, each volume one dollar; publisher, Carl Fischer. Philip Mittell's *Graded Violin Pieces* (Schirmer) are also good; the first volume is entirely in the first position, the second in the first three positions, and each volume costs a dollar. And there is, at seventy-five cents, the *Classical Album of Early Grade Violin Pieces by Famous Composers*, all arranged for the first position; Boston Music Company. Other violin albums are listed in Appendix A and Schirmer's catalog, "Music for String and Wind Instruments," will supply you with endless repertoire, from salon pieces to sonatas and other classic forms. In that catalog you will find listed, not only a wealth of literature for violin and piano, but for piano and bassoon, trombone, clarinet, flute, oboe, trumpet or cornet, viola, cello, and even double-bass.

Speaking of the cello, I would like to mention two albums of great usefulness for amateurs: *Willeke's Violoncello Collection,* selected and edited by Willem Willeke, in two volumes, each $1.50.

## Duets

Piano duets have progressed far from the nineteenth-century days when the musical market was flooded with mediocre transcriptions of symphonies and operatic airs. Today hundreds of good compositions are available for duet-playing, with the balance of difficulty and musical significance nicely adjusted between the two parts. Below is a list of duet albums, ranging from intermediate to difficult:

*Everybody's Favorite Piano Duets.* Amsco. $1.
*Piano Duets the Whole World Plays.* Appleton-Century. $1.25.
*Piano Duets the Whole World Loves.* Willis. 75¢.
*Classical Album: Piano, Four Hands.* G. Schirmer. Twelve original pieces by Haydn, Mozart (a complete sonata for one piano, four hands), Beethoven, Weber, and so on. $1.

*Album of Transcriptions for Piano, Four Hands.* G. Schirmer. $1.25.

*Recital Pieces for Piano, Four Hands.* G. Schirmer. $1.25.

## Two Pianos, Four Hands

In recent years, this form of ensemble playing has attained great artistic heights. Most of the great concerti for piano are arranged with a reduction, for the second piano, of the orchestral accompaniment. But these are for very advanced players, as are the two famous "Suites" for two pianos, one by Arensky and one by Rachmaninoff, each of which contains a delightful waltz movement. There is much two-piano literature of intermediate difficulty and in that connection I mention Schirmer's *Album of Piano Duos* ($1.50) and Harcourt, Brace's *Pieces for Two Pianos, Four Hands—36 Composers Represented* ($5.75).

Vera Brodsky, one of the great duo-pianists, has written a very interesting article on this art which appears, beginning on page 338, in Albert E. Wier's *The Piano—Its History, Makers, Players, and Music* (Longmans, Green). Following this article, which should be read by every pianist wishing to play two-piano music, is a chapter entitled "A Survey of Original and Transcribed Music for Two Pianos," which in turn is followed by a list of the best duo-piano literature extant. The fact that this list covers twenty-one pages of close print is dramatic evidence of the wealth of music available in this form.

## Chamber Music

One of the richest rewards awaiting the amateur pianist who has developed his skill to the intermediate stage is that of playing chamber music with his friends. Often an amateur pianist lives, without knowing it, in proximity to amateur violinists, violists, cellists, and wind-instrument players, all of whom would be as glad as he to get together for *gemütliche* evenings of chamber music. If you live in a city, one way to get in touch with instrumentalists is to leave word with your friends behind the counter in the music store where you buy so many piano scores; just tell them that, like Barkis, you are willing. They'll pass the word on and you might have a group around your piano within the week. Another way is to put a brief item in the Personal Notices column of your local paper. And don't forget: out of your group you can isolate the violinist, violist, and cellist for other evenings of duets and sonatas.

Sylvia Smith, concert pianist and one of the most expert chamber-music performers in New York, has been good enough to give me suggestions, which are incorporated in the paragraphs which follow, about chamber music centering around the piano.

As to repertoire, albums should be used before undertaking the more difficult repertoire of trios, quartets, and quintets. For the trio combination consisting of violin, cello, and piano, Schirmer puts out (in two books, $1.25 each) *Little Masterpieces in Easy Trio Arrangements*, edited by Alexander Barjansky. Also ($2) a *Trio Album—Arrangements of Favorite Melodies*, by Robert Biederman. Also *Our First Trio Book*, six folk airs arranged by Hazel Gertrude Kinscella (75¢).

While on the subject of trios, I might mention that there is repertoire in this form for combinations other than the usual one of violin, cello, and piano: for piano with clarinet and bassoon, clarinet and viola, clarinet and cello, flute and bassoon, flute and cello, oboe and bassoon, oboe and viola, oboe and cello, violin and bassoon, violin and viola, and two violins. See the Schirmer catalog of "Music for String and Wind Instruments" * for compositions in all these combinations.

Among the simplest and most charming trios in the usual combination of violin, cello, and piano are the thirty-one by Haydn. Mozart wrote six for this combi-

* Free on request.

nation and a seventh for clarinet, viola, and piano. There are eleven trios by Beethoven, including one which, though not difficult, is always played with especial reverence: the trio in E flat, which is the master's Op. 1, No. 1. There are two trios by Mendelssohn, including the very popular one in D minor. Chopin wrote a little-known Trio in G minor for which I have been unable to find an opus number; the piano part is, as might be expected, especially interesting. Schubert's two trios—Op. 99 and Op. 100—are technically difficult, but among the best things he wrote. Also difficult is Dvořák's famous "Dumky" Trio, Op. 90; but some chamber-music connoisseurs prefer Dvořák's Op. 65 Trio in F minor. Arensky wrote a charming trio and so did Tchaikovsky. Schumann wrote three. Brahms wrote five, all of them extremely difficult.

The piano quartet literature is more limited. The usual combination is that of violin, viola, cello, and piano. Mozart wrote two delightful piano quartets. Brahms wrote three; Dvořák two; Schumann one, the great quartet in E flat, Op. 47. There is a woodwind-and-piano quartet by Beethoven, also scored (by the composer) for the usual strings and piano; Op. 16, key of E flat.

The usual piano-quintet combination is the string quartet with piano added. Schubert's famous *Forellen*

Quintet, however, is scored for piano, violin, viola, cello, and double bass (a second cello may be substituted for the double bass). In the usual combination, there are quintets by Brahms, Schumann, César Franck, and Dvořák. Piano quintets are without exception "very difficult," technically speaking.

Should you be able to expand your chamber-music group to the size of a small orchestra, you will find much expertly scored material—always including the piano-conductor's part—in Schirmer's "Orchestra and Band Music Catalog." *

A good way for amateurs to plan their evenings is to play from albums for sight reading and pure musical enjoyment, while undertaking one "big" composition at each session, on which the various members of the ensemble have worked at home in the period between meetings.

The amateur pianist developing a chamber-music group will get along better and faster if he observes the following advice from Sylvia Smith. The violinist "starts" any piece with a vigorous nod of his head, and sets tempi with his head and bow arm. But the pianist is the only one with a full score in front of him—all the others have only their own parts and therefore have to count out all measures where they are silent. It is up to

* Free on request.

the pianist, if and when the group comes to a halt, to call out "Let's start from four measures before G." The violinist is, in a sense, the conductor: when there is a change of tempo, the pianist looks at the violinist for the new beat. But, in another sense, the pianist is even more the conductor, for it is up to him to play with very strong rhythm—even with exaggerated rhythm—to keep the group together. The violinist sets the rhythmic pace but the pianist maintains it. Care must be exercised by the pianist here, however, not to play too loud and drown out the others. Most amateur pianists have a tendency to play too loud in chamber music. The pianist must never forget that he is now playing an ensemble, not a solo, instrument. He is always in the background except when carrying the melody. His bass should be solid, but not too loud. He should listen to the other players rather than to himself. When making an "entrance," it should be molded into the general web of sound; it should not be a big moment for the piano and the pianist. Follow all dynamic markings; you achieve only a Pyrrhic victory if you play the notes with accuracy but *ff* where the score reads *pp*. Keeping going counts above all else in amateur ensemble music: never, if you can possibly help it, force the group to stop and start again because of you. Apologies for poor playing should be ruled out at the start; otherwise more time may be spent in excuses for stumbling, stopping, incorrect reading, etc., than in playing. Be good to cellists; there are far fewer cellists than violinists or violists. Therefore be kind to them, and civil; if your cellist is temperamental, humor him; if he is late in an entrance, don't chide him; if he plays well, pat him on the shoulder. Keep him in a good frame of mind and your chances of keeping your chamber-music group intact will improve vastly. As to page turning, only the pianist has a problem. Whoever turns for you should turn the page from the top, so that his arm doesn't obstruct your field of vision; and he should school himself not to get so absorbed in watching the other players that he forgets to turn.

## "Add-a-Part" Records

I would say that the greatest advance for amateur chamber-music players since the invention of their instruments is the idea behind "Add-a-Part" records. Three years ago Fritz Rothschild, Austrian violinist, teacher, and chamber-music authority came to this country and interested the Columbia Recording Company in his idea, which was to record chamber-music works with one part—first violin, second violin, cello, or piano —missing. The records have proved very popular and additions are being made every month. Each record or album includes the missing part written out in full, with a reduction of the other parts, which are played on the record, on the line above. Thus, to quote from the Columbia Records catalog:

"This new and revolutionary approach has solved what has been a major problem in enjoying chamber music, namely organizing well-matched ensembles so that players can learn as they play and listen. Thanks to 'Add-a-Part' records these difficulties no longer exist. Now every musician, amateur or professional, can join in with a highly skilled ensemble and enjoy the art of playing the great chamber-music compositions when and where he wishes. Chamber music players call it a dream come true. The players you need are always there when you need them. And so is the music. By using 'Add-a-Part' records, you not only learn your part at first hand, but—what is more important—you learn your part in relation to the others, and get to understand the fuller meaning and structure of the music as a whole. The record is always patient. You can play and replay it at will. This is the simplest, quickest way to master the art, and enjoy the unending pleasure of playing the world's greatest chamber music in your own home."

Below is a tabulation of "Add-a-Part" records, with piano missing, available as this book goes to press:

## Single Records (easy)

Strauss, *The Blue Danube Waltz* (record #65116) $1.50

Strauss, *Emperor Waltz* (65166) $1.50

Strauss, *Tales from the Vienna Woods* (65167) $1.50

Liszt, *Second Hungarian Rhapsody* (arranged for string quartet and piano, or piano quintet)—(65242) $1.50

Schubert, *Marche militaire* and *Ave Maria* (65233) $1.50

Saint-Saëns, *The Swan;* and Mendelssohn, *On Wings of Song* (65234) $1.50

Brahms, *Waltz;* and Schumann, *Träumerei* (65185) $1

Mozart, Second Movement from the Trio in G, K. 564 (65117) $1.50

## Albums (easy)

Beethoven, Trio in B flat, Opus 11 (Set S–24) $5

Haydn, Trio No. 1 in C (S–19) $3.50

Mozart, Trio in E flat, K. 498 (S–20) $5

Mozart, Sonata for Violin and Piano, K. 296 (S–21) $3.50

## Albums (medium)

Beethoven, Trio in G, Opus 1, No. 2 (S–22) $6.50

Beethoven, Trio in C minor, Opus 1, No. 3 (S–23) $6

Mendelssohn, Trio No. 1 in D minor (S–41) $7.50

Schubert, Quintet in A ("The Trout") (S–26) $8

## Albums (difficult)

Brahms, Piano Quintet in F minor, Op. 34 (S–33) $8
Schubert, Trio No. 1 in B flat, Op. 99 (S–25) $6.50
Schumann, Piano Quintet in E flat, Op. 44 (S–27) $6

It may have surprised you to note that compositions with a long, singing melody line like *The Swan, Ave Maria,* and *On Wings of Song* have been recorded with the piano missing. You may have thought, as I did until I examined these recordings, that they would have been more effective with the violin or cello missing. The fact is, however, that the piano part has been written in so ingeniously—sometimes as accompaniment, sometimes as melody carrier—that these records provide excellent practice in both types of pianism.

It is the hope of Fritz Rothschild, the originator, that "Add-a-Part" clubs will spring up over the country, meeting regularly and exchanging recordings.

## ACKNOWLEDGMENTS

The author expresses grateful thanks for copyright permissions as follows:

TEXT:

The excerpts from the writings of Dr. Josef Hofmann on pages xi, 26, 28, 49, 102–103, and 119–120 are quoted, by permission of the copyright owners, from *Piano Playing with Piano Questions Answered*, by Dr. Josef Hofmann, published and copyrighted 1920 by the Theodore Presser Company.

The following excerpts—pages 9–10 (Paderewski), 14 (Bachaus), 16 (de Pachmann), 49 (Ernest Schelling), 100 (Godowsky), 100–101 (Gabrilowitsch), 105 (Pepito Arriola), 105 (Rachmaninoff), 106 and 126 (Busoni), 107 (Ernest Hutcheson), 131–132 (Lhevinne, Bachaus, Nicholas Rubinstein, Ernest Hutcheson, and de Pachmann), 144 (Hofmann and Busoni), and 145 (Rachmaninoff)—are quoted, by permission of the copyright owners, from *Great Pianists on Piano Playing*, by James Francis Cooke, published and copyrighted 1913 by the Theodore Presser Company.

## Acknowledgments

The excerpts on pages xv and 20 (Anton Rubinstein) and page 111 (Liszt) are quoted, by permission of the copyright owners, from *Free Artist* by Catherine Drinker Bowen, published and copyrighted by Random House.

MUSIC:

The extract on page 61 from Debussy's *Clair de lune* (copyright 1905) is printed by permission of the copyright owners: Jean Jobert, Paris, and Elkan-Vogel, Inc., Philadelphia.

The extract on pages 64–65 from Debussy's *La Fille aux cheveux de lin* (copyright 1910) is printed by permission of the copyright owners: Durand et Cie., Paris, and Elkan-Vogel, Inc., Philadelphia.

The extract on pages 86 and 88 from Palmgren's *May Night* is printed by permission of the copyright owners, the Boston Music Company.

# BOOKS CONSULTED

*Great Pianists on Piano Playing.* James Francis Cooke.
Theodore Presser Co., Philadelphia.

*Piano Playing with Piano Questions Answered.* Josef Hofmann. Presser.

*The Act of Touch in All Its Diversity.* Tobias Matthay.
Longmans, Green.

*The Act of Musical Concentration.* Tobias Matthay. Oxford University Press, London.

*On Memorizing.* Tobias Matthay. Oxford University Press.
London.

*The Principles of Pianoforte Practice.* James Friskin.
H. W. Gray Co.

*How to Play the Piano.* Mark Hambourg. George H.
Doran Co.

*How to Play and Teach Debussy.* Maurice Dumesnil.
Schroeder and Gunther

*The Piano—Its History, Makers, Players, and Music.*
Albert E. Wier. Longmans, Green.

*The Paderewski Memoirs.* Ignace Jan Paderewski and
Mary Lawton. Scribners.

*Leschetizky as I Knew Him.* Ethel Newcomb. Appleton-Century.

*Theodor Leschetizky.* Annette Hullah. John Lane, London.

*Free Artist.* Catherine Drinker Bowen. Random House.

*Teresa Carreño.* Marta Milinowski. Yale University Press.


## BOOKS OF TECHNICAL STUDIES CONSULTED

*51 Exercises.* Brahms. Breitkopf & Härtel, Leipzig.

*School of Scales and Double Notes for the Piano.* Moritz Moszkowski. Boosey, Hawkes, Belwin, Inc., New York.

*Mastering the Scales and Arpeggios.* James Francis Cooke. Presser.

*The Chopin Etudes,* edited by Arthur Friedheim. G. Schirmer.

*Chopin 12 Studies Op. 10.* Students' Edition. Alfred Cortot. Oliver Ditson Co., Boston.

*Chopin 12 Studies Op. 25.* Students' Edition. Alfred Cortot. Oliver Ditson.

*Piano Studies in Modern Idiom.* Katherine Ruth Heyman. Winthrop Rogers, Ltd., London.

*Exercises for Independence of the Fingers.* I. Philipp. G. Schirmer.

*The Virtuoso Pianist.* C. L. Hanon. G. Schirmer.

*Technical Variants on Hanon's Exercises for the Pianoforte.* Orville A. Lindquist. Arthur P. Schmidt Co., Boston.

*Double Third Scales, Their Fingering and Practice.*
Tobias Matthay. Arthur P. Schmidt Co.

*50 Chopin Studien.* Leopold Godowsky. R. und W. Leinau,
Berlin.

## ABOUT THE AUTHOR

*Charles Cooke has been a member of the staff of* The
New Yorker *since 1930, specializing in musical, theat-
rical, and circus stories. He has interviewed such great
pianists as Horowitz, Hofmann, Rosenthal, Brailowsky, and Schnabel. He numbers several concert pianists
among his personal friends. He is the author of one
novel,* Big Show, *and of many short stories. His hobby
is playing the piano for pleasure.*